Debby Brown

D0397909

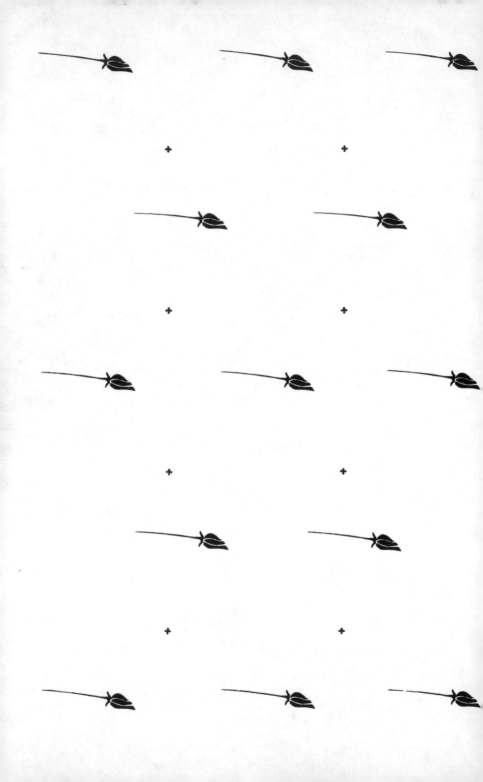

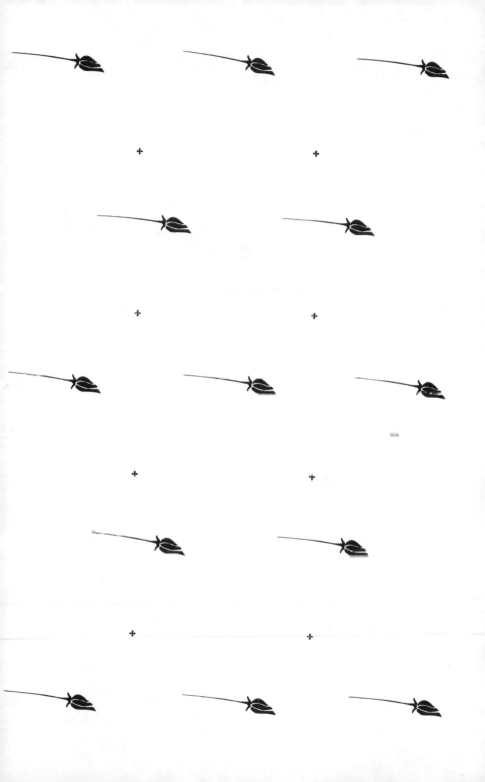

+++

LOVE *and* MARRIAGE

++

LOVE *and*

Introduction by Alvin F. Poussaint, M.D.

DOUBLEDAY
New York London Toronto Sydney Auckland

+++

MARRIAGE

BILL
COSBY

A Doubleday Book
Published by Doubleday, a division of
Bantam Doubleday Dell Publishing Group, Inc.
666 Fifth Avenue, New York, New York 10103

Doubleday and the portrayal of an anchor
with a dolphin are trademarks of
Doubleday, a division of Bantam Doubleday Dell
Publishing Group, Inc.

Library of Congress Cataloging-in-Publication Data

Cosby, Bill, 1937–
    Love and marriage / Bill Cosby ; introduction by Alvin F.
Poussaint. — 1st ed.
        p. cm.
    ISBN 0-385-24664-1
    1. Love—Anecdotes. 2. Marriage—Anecdotes. 3. Love—
Humor. 4. Marriage—Humor.   I. Title.
    BF575.L8C67   1989
    306.7'0207—dc19   88-35242
                                                                        CIP

FIRST EDITION

OG

For Camille
forever

+++

*My warm thanks to Ralph Schoenstein,
whose wonderful
voice has joined mine in this book as it did
in* Fatherhood *and* Time Flies.

✛✛

CONTENTS

+++

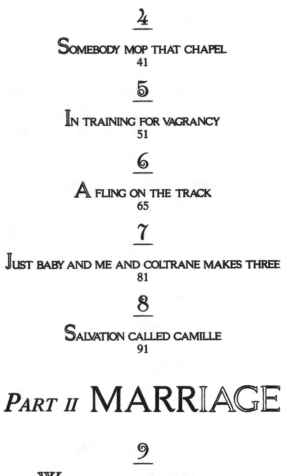
+++

+++

I have been married for twenty-five years, but I am not an authority on marriage and this is not a marital textbook. These are just some Cliffs Notes, not from Heathcliff but Bill, just some memories and reflections about how I wandered in the sexual wilderness awhile and then found the best thing that ever happened to me, Camille Hanks Cosby.

And I am certainly not an authority on love because there are no authorities on love, just those who've had luck with it and those who haven't. In finding Camille, I drew to an inside straight, queen high.

++

LOVE and MARRIAGE

++

Introduction

by Alvin F. Poussaint, M.D.

Bill Cosby begins this comic caper about romance and matrimony with a description of his erotic awakening in the inner city of Philadelphia, where he grew up. The story has a familiar ring; we have all floundered and lost our innocence during our awkward, adolescent "love" encounters. *Love and Marriage* is about the journey most of us have taken down lovers' lane, driven by impulses that feel titillating but are often as mystifying as they are overwhelming. Cosby says love is "the only subject that no one has ever been able to study for."

Love and marriage may sometimes go together like the proverbial horse and carriage, but that—you'd better believe—is an oversimplification. A person can certainly have one without the other, yet it's a blessing indeed when love and marriage can be merged by ordinary mortals as debonairly as Cosby brings it off on his hit television show. The display of love between Clair and Cliff Huxtable is particularly engaging, their affection and caring palpably genuine. Cosby isn't just putting us on; he is well aware of the ingredients essential to a successful partnership—insight based to some degree, no doubt, on his enduring relationship with his real-life spouse, Camille.

However, prior to his meeting Camille, when Cosby was in his mid-twenties, his ambiguous search for "love" was plagued with numerous—sometimes amusing—mishaps. America's number one husband and father received his romantic initiation in a city where hip adolescent males aimed to "score," for their pleasure, of course, but also to gather ego-boosting macho points. Cosby notes that his early quest for "love" was beset by chaos because of his preoccupation with female anatomy.

No one can fault Cosby or his buddies for their dilemma; nature endows us with sexual instincts that frequently border on the uncontrollable. As if that were not enough, we are constantly bombarded with sexual stimulation from television, movies, music, magazines, and individuals who are obsessed with looking "sexy." No wonder sexual development begins earlier in childhood than most of us realize and often peaks during the early teens.

+++

Cosby humorously recalls coming of age, marked by his first wet dream. He tells of trying to hide the evidence of his new manhood from his parents by hurriedly washing his sheets, and of being discovered —to his great chagrin.

Cosby doesn't say whether he had previously known about nocturnal emissions. Many of the would-be young studs and foxes he describes were seriously misinformed about love and sex. Today, despite great advances in sexual knowledge, and the lifting of taboos on disseminating that knowledge, too many children remain misinformed. Parents and those responsible for school curricula are still uncomfortable with the prospect of teaching children about normal sexual development. Youngsters who rely heavily on street folklore about sex often make foolish and self-destructive decisions.

Adolescents—and many adults as well—tend to be attracted by physical characteristics rather than by the more important personal qualities. They "go crazy" over individuals who are cute, handsome, or pretty, and may fall instantly and totally "in love."

A "loved one" may be a projection of a person's own ideal image. In an intense romance, the partner may be so blinded by passion that he or she may misperceive the true traits of the loved one. Cosby wryly notes: "Since self-deception is the heart of falling in love, perhaps the best sex education for a boy is not studying drawings of reproductive systems but simply learning to lie to himself." Incidentally, some psychologists consider falling in love a "benign psychosis"—a simple form of mental illusion. Since "being in love" can severely distort good sense, experienced adults warn the young of its perils.

Unfortunately, many smitten youngsters engage in early and irresponsible sexual activity, thereby facing many risks, foremost among them contracting sexually transmitted diseases, including life-threatening AIDS. Still children themselves, girls who become pregnant face the ordeal of abortion or the hardship and poverty of premature, single parenthood. Dreadful suffering is inflicted in the name of love and sex when young people do not comprehend the almost inevitable consequences of their ignorance.

On the other hand, positive realistic approaches to romance can enhance the prospects for a happy love and marriage experience as opposed to one that ends in misery and divorce. Most psychologists believe that young people should engage in social activities with a variety of partners to determine what sort of person they *really* like and are compatible with. We may be wising up to the fact that early and hasty commitments to love relationships are risky: data indicates that more people today are waiting until they are well into their twenties to marry.

Marriage at a later age can offer certain benefits.

Both men and women are apt to exercise more mature judgment in their choice of partners and to be reasonably secure in their jobs and careers. Their education completed, couples usually achieve a measure of financial security and independence that is almost impossible to attain during the teen years. The cost of housing and basic necessities, plus the expense of raising children, can put enormous strains on a marriage; poverty itself frequently precipitates separation and divorce.

The bonds of love are, unfortunately, vulnerable to environmental and social stresses. Couples eagerly commit to the vow "For better for worse . . . in sickness and in health," but many retreat when the going gets rough. It is certainly naïve to expect any love partnership to continue smoothly without problems arising along the way. When Cosby describes disagreements he and Camille have had, we realize that even happy marriages are subject to periods of stress that can push a relationship to the breaking point.

In every marriage, the relationship and the individuals change over time. Cosby alludes to these changes when he says about marriage, "Yes, it's wonderful at the beginning when your life together is a romantic high." Social scientists report that most long-term relationships undergo a series of predictable stages: infatuation and idealization of the partner; cooling down, disappointment, moving toward a more realistic relationship; becoming a parent and pursuing a career, often called the stage of productivity; redefining the relationship and its goals while raising children to maturity; and finally, the empty nest or post-parenting stage, called a period of reintegration of the marriage. As in any general categorization, passage through these stages is variable and may not conform exactly to the outlined progression. The point is that marriage is a living—not a static—process. Cosby observes, "With all the irregular rhythms that pulse between a husband and wife, the wonder is that any couple can sustain the glow of romance."

As marriages pass through normal developmental stages, they sometimes hit snags that may appear to be fatal. For instance, if, after a year or two, the intensity of sexual passion diminishes, it is not necessarily a cause for alarm. The partners may be settling down to a less infatuated but deeper and quieter period of love. Then again, they may have to work a bit harder at maintaining a good sex life. Showing affection in other ways—with hugs, kisses, and overall attentiveness—may be more important and sustaining at such a time. People who expect everlasting sexual ecstasy in marriage are usually disillusioned and feel as if the love has been lost. Breaking up the marriage at this stage may indicate that the partners lack a mature understanding of natural developments in long-term relationships and marriage.

✛✛

Another important transition, often a cause of marital stress, is the birth of a child. Cosby discusses at length the effect of his children on his marriage. New parents may resent the constraints on their freedom to have fun or to pursue careers. The routines of daily living change dramatically; even the privacy for sexual intimacy, once taken for granted, is disturbed. Children bring taxing new demands and responsibilities to even the best-adjusted parents. We know that raising a family can affect us in mysterious ways, altering our personalities as well as our philosophy of life. Our values may change as we face the awesome responsibility of guiding children through a difficult and changing world. Although the addition of a child heralds a marital adjustment, it is also an occasion of great joy.

Cosby, on his television show as in real life, has five children, and it is obvious that they have brought delight to both his make-believe and real marriages. The shared love for children, even in times of trial, has perhaps no equal in the emotional realm of bonding and intimacy; it can deeply enrich a relationship. Shared intimate experiences in many areas is what adds "that extra something" to the routine of marriage; a different quality of closeness evolves as couples share life's many ups and downs.

A word of warning, however: closeness thrives best in an atmosphere in which the partners accord mutual respect and accept individual differences. Frequent confrontations, leading to bitter stalemates or the holding of grudges, can destroy the communication and intimacy that are critical to any lasting partnership. Cosby suggests that because partners owe it to themselves to guard against such tendencies, they should practice compromising and negotiating conflict: "I realized how important it is for each partner in a marriage to make adjustments. One of mine is agreeing to live in a minimum security prison."

Cosby's down-to-earth views on love and matrimony will make every reader laugh—and reminisce.

Preface

—

JANE RUSSELL WAS NO PG-13

I was born in 1937, when the mission of a man was to slay the beast and plow the field, a considerable challenge in North Philadelphia; and when the mission of a woman was to cook a man's food, wash his clothes, and be a contented bystander in bed. How medieval that America now seems, an America where a boy named Bill Cosby played all day with his muscles in high, his brain in low, and his glands in neutral. In my preteen years in postwar America, girls to me were merely a minor bother, like a lost skate key or a mosquito bite. Unlike a boy of ten today, who primps for a dance while being transported by the poetry of a ballad called "I Want Your Sex," I never thought about bowling over girls—just about knocking them down if they were near the

++

playing field. And a darkened living room, of course, was never one of my fields.

I tell you all this at the start of the book so that you will have a historical fix on the man you are hearing from, a man who did not learn the truth about human reproduction until the late forties; and when I finally got this comical information, it was from the University of the Gutter and not from my grade school hygiene class, where even the Pope would have been bored. I remember a day when I was ten or eleven and an older boy said with a casual smirk, "You know why my sister got thrown out of sewing class?"

"Because she needled the teacher?" I replied.

"No, because she couldn't *mend*strate."

The joke flew right by me, for it seemed to me that mending was only one part of sewing. Even if his sister couldn't mend straight, she still might have been able to do a lovely job of cross-stitching.

Such innocence had to fade, of course, and mine began fading in a movie house that was playing a new picture called *The Outlaw*. There I saw a considerable portion of an actress named Jane Russell, who looked like the poster girl for National Nursing Mothers Month; and something told me that this was not the kind of female at whom you threw elbows, jelly beans, and water bombs.

My budding awareness of sex came not just from

Jane Russell's billowing blouse, for about the same time other media also were sounding a wake-up call to my hormones. At the suggestion of my friend who told the bawdy sewing joke, I took my hands off a basketball long enough to pick up a book called *God's Little Acre*. My reading in those days had been basically a blend of comic books and highway signs; in fact, *God's Little Acre* may have been the first thing that I ever read in hard covers; but what an enlightening look at how people behaved south of Philadelphia. *God's Little Acre* was not about the location for a new church.

Now deeply devoted to the literary life, I broadened my reading to include nonfiction in 1948. That year, when I was eleven, I passed up Proust to settle down with a work called *Sexual Behavior in the Human Male* by three Indiana doctors, one of whom was named Kinsey. The book was quite long, but it happened to be published in Philadelphia and I believed in supporting the local arts.

And so, you now know the ancient culture that shaped the man who is starting to talk to you about matters of the heart and below. A boy today would read the Kinsey Report at the age of nine (if he wanted something a little less sexual than the evening news) and then tell his mother where the book required updating; but I was a boy who, at nineteen, still felt that the peak of erotica was Kim Novak put-

++

ting blankets on the shivering Sinatra in *The Man with the Golden Arm,* a scene that could play on "Sesame Street" today.

In my twenties, I gallantly paid the check for every woman I took to dinner. How many light-years that was from the average dinner date of 1989, where the woman not only is liable to pick up the check, but often has to look behind her condoms for her credit card. My boyhood was so quaint that I was fourteen before I could tell a condom from a carp: in my early years, I saw many condoms as they floated at the waterfront, but I thought that they were dead fish. It was a long time before I knew how sailors swam upstream to spawn.

But eventually I learned, not just about the silly mechanics of sex but also about the sweet madness of love, about the one virus that will never have a vaccine. And I learned about women, but not too much.

In this book, I will share with you my lifelong study of women and love. I cannot, however, claim to have gotten an A myself in this course. In fact, I'm still taking it pass-fail; but my teacher, Camille Cosby, thinks that I do have a chance to finally learn the material before the century is out.

+++

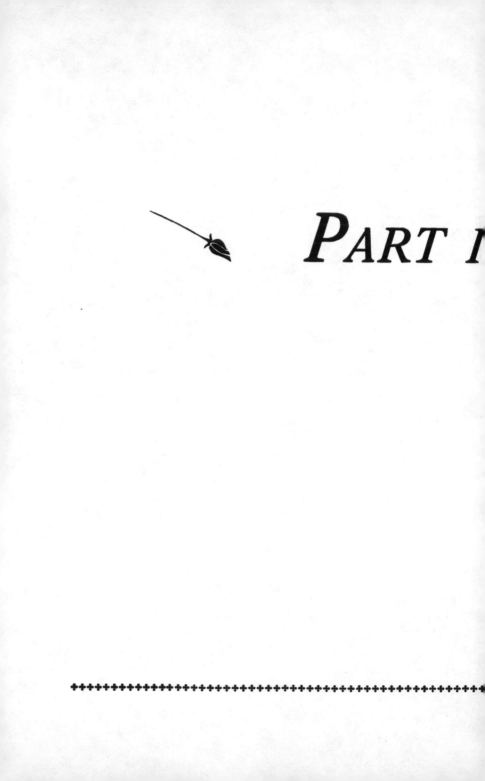

PART I

LOVE

1

———

PRESCRIPTION FROM DR. KINSEY

Since self-deception is the heart of falling in love, perhaps the best sex education for a boy is not studying drawings of reproductive systems but simply learning to lie to himself. The first time that I can remember lying to myself, I was eight years old and playing in a friend's house. His parents were out working and my friend Tom and I were spending the evening jumping from bed to bed. Many men, of course, have enjoyed the sport of jumping from bed to bed, but rarely in sneakers.

After a while, Tom and I decided to take a break and go down to the kitchen to raid the ice box. Not the refrigerator: the ice box, for this was 1945, a time when radioactivity meant an evening of programs and a liberated woman was one who had just come

++

out of jail and Victrola was not an Italian girl but a machine for playing breakable records. Japan had just surrendered, and from time to time my mother was ready to give up on *me,* especially when I managed to leave footprints on her pillow.

And so, on this gymnastic evening, Tom and I went downstairs and made a turn toward the kitchen. As we did, we passed a small living room; and there we saw Tom's older brother George—he was at least seventeen—kissing his girlfriend on a couch. Tom and I looked at each other with big grins, for kissing anything but your aunt at Christmas was a comical thing to do. If faces had been meant to kiss each other, they would not have been given noses.

Suddenly, however, the scene turned from the comical to the bizarre because we saw that the girl had her *tongue* in George's mouth and *George's* tongue was misplaced too. Feeling as though I were part of a National Geographic expedition to a primitive culture, I remembered a fundamental law of the civilized world: every mouth should have just one tongue and that one should be its own.

What could that girl's tongue possibly have been *doing* in George's mouth? It was a silly place to look for a snack. As you see, not only was I a rotten ichthyologist in identifying fish at the waterfront, but I was also a rotten entomologist in the living room: the first time I came across the birds and the bees in actual flight, I couldn't identify the formation.

As Tom and I watched those two tongues wandering around in the wrong mouths, we felt sick. After about a minute of observation, our heads spinning in dismay, we turned and went out into the backyard.

"That's it!" I told Tom. "I'm *really* disgusted with girls now. I'm never gonna hit another one."

"Or even steal another one's lunch," said Tom.

"Or even hit one with a jelly bean."

"I never liked 'em to begin with."

"Let's make a pact," I said. "The first girl who ever puts her tongue in our mouth, we give it right back to her—and tell her the only place to serve tongue is in a delicatessen!"

And that was the first time I ever lied to myself, for deep inside of me I knew that the scene on that couch involved something delightful.

In those G-rated years when I couldn't recognize the birds and the bees, girls were a kind of dopey enemy to me and my friends, one to be mocked and rejected and occasionally knocked down. If a girl wandered on to a football field where I was playing, I might make knocking her down part of my fly pattern, for a girl was only an honorary human being; and if my roller skating assumed a certain grand sweep, a girl or two might hit the cement, not an unfitting position for such a lesser part of humanity. In my relations with girls at the age of eight, I never broke hearts, I merely tore skin. Girls simply had to understand that boys did not sit quietly on the floor feeding dolls: boys practiced the violence that was so essential to their becoming men. For example, the Fourth of July was my favorite holiday, not because I was a patriot but because I was deeply attached to explosions.

There were definite rules for how prepubescent boys were supposed to behave in their maleness club, just as there were rules for the behavior of girls in their society of untouchables. Have you ever seen the outside of an elementary school at recess? It looks like a documentary about stags in heat: boys are tackling each other and pummeling each other and generally polishing their flair for mayhem, while the girls are standing nearby and watching the scene as if visiting a zoo. Any girl who broke the rules of her club and joined in the violence was called a tomboy; but any boy who broke the rules of *his* club and looked down on the pounding of kidneys was called less distinguished things. "William's Doll" is a fine song for our liberated time. In the forties, however, William's doll meant only someone who played with William as much as he played with her.

Although my mother was a female, she was not a member of this silly enemy called girls. In fact, I was proud of her and considered myself an assistant father in protecting her. As a preteen boy, I had fantasies about killing people who messed with my mother: I was the John Wayne of North Philadelphia, constantly ready to draw on a mother messer. And I also fantasized about having money (a quarter would have qualified as a portfolio for me then) and having a house, where I would live with my wife and protect her from runaway streetcars and savage beasts.

Even though American women had just finished spending four years building bombers in defense plants, those were still the days of the helpless female. Moreover, I never believed that women really built bombers in those defense plants. Maybe they waxed the floors and tidied up the cockpits, but surely nothing more, for women were never involved in any kind of warfare. They never felt the love of destruction that moved me and my friends to throw dolls against walls to see if their heads would come off. Our own heads, of course, were not screwed on too tightly either.

Suddenly, almost overnight, a grand transformation takes place in that student of carnage called a boy: it's "Good morning, glands." Suddenly, you don't want to knock a girl down, you want to bowl her over. Suddenly, you lose interest in scarring her

++

knees and turn your attention to making an impact on her heart.

The girl, of course, is thoroughly bewildered by your entrance into the human race. However, she has waited so long for you to join it that she may already have decided to find another species, one that hasn't tortured her since the age of four, one that wants to give her roses and not strawberries from falls on cement.

This miraculous male metamorphosis begins with a dream that is not quite as lofty as Martin Luther King's, a dream with both mental and physical parts. The mental part involves changing your attitude and the physical part involves changing your sheets.

On the memorable night when it happened to me, something strangely wonderful possessed me and even set off sounds. In *Guys and Dolls*, the heroine describes her first heady rush of love by saying that if she were a bell she'd be ringing. Well, in my dream, I *did* hear ringing; and the following day, I wanted to reach out and touch someone. In the lineup at school, I now saw girls as if for the first time: objects of derision had become objects of desire. The day before, I had knocked Joyce Anderson down while catching a pass; but today the pass was at her: I gave her my most fetching smile, which made her think that something had slipped in my tiny mind.

♥

Beneath my smile at Joyce Anderson was a body that had recently showered, for the physical part of the dream had been to awaken in a sticky situation and feel a profound desire to help your mother with the laundry by washing your sheets at once. What a challenge this laundering can be for the boy who has just awakened from an overnight arrival at puberty.

I remember the morning I came downstairs all dressed for school at six-thirty, carrying my pajamas and sheets. I should have been carrying my mattress too because the manhood had gone through to it, but I'd decided to have an accidental fire in the mattress later on. As I reached the foot of the stairs, I ran into my father, who graciously played along with my domestic nobility.

"Doing some laundry, Bill?" he said.

"Yes, Dad," I replied. "Mom has such a heavy load."

"What a good boy! What a wonderful son! How many sons help their mothers with the laundry even before they sit down to breakfast?"

The answer, of course, was every son who awakened as a sperm bank.

In those ancient days, my family had a big washing machine with an agitator action (that never could have become as agitated as *I* was), a clanking contraption that you pushed up to the kitchen sink. Doing undercover washing in this machine was about as easy as doing undercover hand grenade testing in the hall; and so, I took my embarrassing laundry down to the basement sink, where I added last night's underwear for camouflage.

In this sink, I quickly went to work with a bar of soap to remove the telltale stains of maturity. There was, however, a small flaw in my plan: we had no drier in that basement, so my sheets and pajamas ended up not only clean but also wet. Figuring that they had the entire day to dry, and hoping for a warm desert wind to start blowing through the house, I took them back upstairs to my room.

Had I been a spy who operated with such style, the enemy would soon have been offering me the menu for my last meal.

"Bill," said my mother after finding my soggy sheets, "if you want to help me with the laundry, why not go all the way? You can't put wet sheets on your bed unless you plan to sleep in a raincoat."

"I just don't know how to *do* it, Mom," I said. "I guess it takes a mother's touch to get them dry."

"No, it takes the line in the backyard."

A few minutes later, I hung up the sheets in the yard and I wanted to hang myself beside them, for all the neighbors were watching me and having a good laugh about my hormones. But what can *any* boy do with his sheets after such a momentous night? It's a harder disposal problem than nuclear waste. If only a boy could tell his mother and father about sex.

+++

2

AS THE BOTTLE SPINS

Puberty causes the changing of considerably more than your sheets. I remember that puberty inspired me to brush my hair so hard that I almost exposed the area where my brains should have been. The moment my glands kicked in, I began to brush my hair a hundred times a day so that not a single strand was out of place for the girls I now wanted to impress. I shined my own shoes, I cut the tiny hanging strings off the frayed parts of my collar, and, in a stunning blend of vanity and vapidness, I even began to flaunt my eyelashes, which were particularly long. Before puberty, I had actually trimmed these lashes because women had said I looked like a girl; but now I was grooming them with a toothbrush and wondering if girls would prefer them from the front or the side.

+++

"Have you seen Bill blink?" I could hear a pretty girl say.

"Oh, yes," her unattractive friend would reply. "That blinking Bill drives me wild."

"Do you prefer his lashes from the front or the side?"

"They're hairy enchantment from any direction."

My escalating grooming went far beyond just polishing my lashes or changing my clothes two or three times a week. The first thing every morning, instead of taking to the streets to play ball, I took a bath; and, as I soaked, I thought about the way that I'd be playing ball from now on: not to score for victory but to score with girls. I had already begun to lose the concentration needed for sporting success. Now, when I left a huddle, I sometimes forgot the play because I was thinking about a face on the sidelines; and now, when I got a bunt sign, I ignored it and thought long ball, for no girl ever fell for a bunter; and now, when I dribbled to the top of the key, even if I was being triple-teamed, I never thought about passing off, for girls got no tingles from your assists.

All those sporting moves were attempts to win girls from afar. At parties, however, I had chances to win girls by playing games *with* them, games like Spin the Bottle, a name that brings wistful smiles to people over thirty-five; but it also brings bewilderment, for I am yet to find anyone who remembers precisely how it was played. Everyone remembers that the girls and boys sat in a circle on the floor, one of them spun the bottle, and then had to kiss the person to whom the bottle was pointing. But was it considered winning or losing if the bottle pointed to someone you didn't like or someone who wanted to be a nun? And did you always have to kiss the person the bottle was pointing to or were you allowed to look at her face, cry "Foul!" and spin again?

Most of us in early puberty were fit to be priests and nuns because we knew as much about how to play at sex as we did about how to play jai alai; and so, at these semierotic games, most of us faked it and pretended that a quick kiss on the cheek had made the earth move. All that had moved, of course, was the furniture when we formed the big circle that left us trembling on the brink of adulthood.

Even if you were one of the ten or fifteen kids in Philadelphia who were sexually poised, the bottle never seemed to point to the person you wanted to kiss, but always to her homely best friend. It was better to try your luck at Post Office, another game whose rules are lost to the memories of most adults. How did you decide which of the players would be carrying the mail? Was the delivery always made in front of everyone else? Did the mail ever go astray? How often was it junk mail?

✦✦✦

The kissing game I most vividly remember was called Seven Minutes in Heaven. The two players went into a closet, where they were supposed to find celestial bliss by spending seven minutes kissing. Of course, there was no shot clock in the closet: just a boy and girl who wondered why they were feeling less passion than fear. Therefore, Seven Minutes in Heaven often became five in camphor balls. However, it was good to have at least three or four minutes away from the crowd because you and the girl needed that time to make up your story about ecstasy in the overcoats. And if the two of you were able to make up your story in less time, then you had a few minutes to just sit down in the galoshes and make sophisticated talk.

"Nice weather we're having in the closet."

"Yes, it's been a lovely spring in here."

At the time that I tip-toed into puberty, American movie screens were showing a wholesome kind of interspecies sex: the cowboy kissed his horse more often than he kissed his girl. I never was able to understand such veterinary romance because the girls that the cowboys avoided kissing were always beautiful. I, however, encountered two or three girls who *looked* like horses—although, to be fair, I'm sure I struck *them* as something closer to Don Quixote than Don Juan.

How quaint were those cinematic images of sex

that accompanied me into puberty, images as sensuous as *Little Women*. Today, even prepubescent children are watching anatomical lessons on MTV, a channel that my father would have been arrested for watching in 1947; and my twelve-year-old has already played both home and road games of Spin the Bottle. I nervously hope that she hasn't played a new game I just heard about called Cops and Robbers. In this one, the boy playing it is a policeman whose mission is to search for an important document; and the most likely place for the document to be hidden is in a girl's blouse.

Such a search and seizure lacks a certain tenderness: shoving your hand toward a girl's bra to dig out an imaginary document is not the most romantic approach. It is better to leave this playing field and make your approach to one special girl in a more leisurely way; and this was how I tried to do it in my postpubescent years—in a way sometimes so leisurely that it seemed to take months or even years before I got a kiss.

The kiss: that was everything in those days. Because my generation saw no horizontal sex on big or small screens, the kiss was all-important for us freshly minted young men. That was the ultimate thrill: being alone with a girl and making it all the way to her lips while you were dizzy from her smile and her smell.

✦✦✦

I can't remember where I have left my glasses, but I can still remember the smell of the first girl I ever fell in love with when I was twelve: a blend of Dixie Peach pomade on her hair and Pond's cold cream on her skin; together they were honeysuckle for me. And just as heady as her scent was the thought that I was in love with the only girl in the world for me and would marry her and take care of her forever in a palace in North Philadelphia. Because I wanted to make a wondrous impression on this girl, grooming was suddenly important to me. Before puberty, happiness in appearance for me was pants that didn't fall down and a football that stayed pumped; but now I started taking three long baths a day and washing my own belt until it was white and shining my shoes until I could see in them a face that was ready for romance.

The first time I saw her, she was crossing the street to the school yard and for one golden moment our eyes met. Well, maybe the moment was closer to bronze because she made no response. But at least she had seen me, just about the way that she saw lampposts, hydrants, and manholes. Or was there something more? I began to dream; and later that day, when I was playing with the boys in the yard, it seemed that she was looking at me and the world was suddenly a better place, especially Twelfth and Girard.

However, we still never talked, but just traded silent unsmiling looks whenever we passed. For several days, just her look was enough of a lift for me; but a higher altitude was coming, for one night at a party, we met and I actually danced with her. Now I was certain that I was in love and was going to win her.

I began my conquest with a combination of sporting skill and hygiene: I made my jump shots and my baths as dazzling as they could be. Oddly enough, however, although I saw her every day at school and on the weekends too, I never spoke to her. I had what was considered one of the faster mouths in Philadelphia, but I still wasn't ready to talk to her because I feared rejection. I feared:

COSBY: I like you very much. Will you be my girlfriend?

GODDESS: *(Doing a poor job of suppressing a laugh)* I'd rather have some cavities filled.

All I did, therefore, was adore her in silent cleanliness. Each Sunday night, I took a bath and then prepared my shirt and pants for display to her. On Monday morning, I took another bath (Bill the Baptist, I should have been called) and then brushed my hair,

my shoes, and my eyelashes and went outside to
await the pang of another silent passage.

At last, deciding that I could no longer live this
way, I sat down one Sunday night and wrote a note
that was almost to her. It was to her constant girlfriend and it said:

> *Please don't tell her, but find out what she
> thinks of me.*
>
> *Bill*

The following morning, I slipped the note to the
girlfriend and began the longest wait of my life.

Two agonizing days later, the girlfriend slipped me
an answer, but I put it into my pocket unread. For
hours, I carried it around, afraid to read it because I
didn't happen to be in the mood for crushing rejection that day. At last, however, I summoned the courage to open the note and read:

> *She thinks you're cute.*

Not even malaria could have taken my temperature
to where it went. I had been called many things, but
cute was never one of them.

And even lovelier fever lay ahead, for the next time
I saw her, she smiled at me, I smiled at her, and then
I composed my next winged message to her friend:

+++

I think she's cute too. Does she ever talk about me?

The answer to this one came return mail and it sounded like something by Keats:

She talks about you a lot. She knows it when you come around her.

And the angels sang! Imagine: she actually *knew* it when I came around her! The fact that she also knew it when gnats came around her in no way dampened my ecstasy.

And so, we continued to smile as we passed, while I planned my next move. My Western Union style had clearly been charming the pants off her (so to speak) and now I launched my most courageous question yet:

Does she have a boyfriend?

When I opened the answer the next day in school, the air left me faster than it left the *Hindenburg:*

Yes.

Trying to recover from this deflation, I told myself that I was still cute. I was the cutest man in second place. But perhaps my beloved wasn't aware of the glory she kept passing by. Once more, I sat down and wrote:

> *How much longer do you think she'll be going with him? And when she's finished with him, can I be next?*

Note the elegance and dignity of my appeal. My dignity, however, did have some trouble with the reply:

> *She thinks she's going to break up with him in about a week, but she promised Sidney she would go with him next.*

Suddenly, my aching heart found itself at the end of a line. But it was like a line at a bank: I knew it was leading to a payoff. I also knew that I could cream Sidney in cuteness.

Once she had made the transition to Sidney, I patiently began waiting for her to get sick of him. I had to be careful not to rush the illness because Sidney belonged to a tough gang and there was a chance that I might not be walking around too well when the time came for me to inherit her.

And then, one magnificent morning, I received the magic words:

++

She would like to talk to you.

I wrote back to see if she would wait until I had finished duty at my post as a school crossing guard. Yes, she would wait; I could walk her home. We were going steady now; and how much more torrid our passion would be when I began to *talk* to her.

At last, the words came and I chose them with care. As I walked her home from school, I reached into my reservoir of romantic thoughts, smiled at her soulfully, and said, "How you doing?"

Her response was equally poetic: "All right."

"So we're going steady now?"

"You want to?"

"Yeah. Give me your books."

And now, as if our relationship were not already in the depths of desire, I plunged even deeper by saying, "You wanna go to a movie on Saturday?"

"Why not?"

There might have been reasons. Some people were looking at us now because she was so beautiful, people possibly wondering what she was doing with me; but I knew that I was someone special to be the love of a vision like this, no matter how nearsighted that vision might be.

When we reached her door, I said, "Well, I'll see you Saturday."

"Right," she replied as only she could say it.

✦✦

"What time?"

"One o'clock."

When this day of days finally arrived, I took her to a theater where I think the admission was a dime. As we took our seats for the matinee, two basic thoughts were in my mind: not to sit in gum and to be a gentleman.

Therefore, I didn't hold her hand. Instead, I put my arm around the top of her seat in what I felt was a smooth opening move. Unfortunately, it was less a move toward love than toward gangrene: with my blood moving uphill, my arm first began to tingle and then to ache. I could not, however, take the arm down and let my blood keep flowing because such a lowering would mean I didn't love her; so I left it up there, its muscles full of pain, its fingertips full of needlepoints.

Suddenly, this romantic agony was enriched by a less romantic one: I had to go to the bathroom. Needless to say, I couldn't let her know about this urge, for great lovers never did such things. The answer to "Romeo, Romeo, wherefore art thou, Romeo?" was not "In the men's room, Julie."

What a prince of passion I was at this moment: my arm was dead, my bladder was full, and I was out of money too; but I desperately needed an excuse to move, so I said, "You want some popcorn?"

"No," she said.

"Fine, I'll go get some."

When I tried to move, every part of me could move except my arm: it was dead. I reached over and pulled it down with the other one, trying to be as casual as a man could be when pulling one of his arms with the other one.

"What's the matter?" she said.

"Oh, nothing," I replied. "I'm just taking both of my arms with me."

A few minutes later, as I came out of the bathroom, I was startled to meet her: she was coming from the bathroom *too.* How good it was to find another thing that we had in common. With empty bladders and full hearts, we returned to our seats to continue our love.

3

DID YOU GET ANY?

Although my first love and I did nothing more sensuous than hold hands, my peers in puberty soon were tempting me with the lure of other female parts. One afternoon, while I was tossing a ball with my friend Pee Wee, he said, "You're goin' with Rosemary, huh?"

"*Yeah*," I replied with pride.

"Well, did you get any yet?"

"Any *what?*"

"You know, man."

"No, man. What?"

"J-o-n-e-s."

"No," I piously said. "I don't do that kind of thing."

"You mean to tell me if a chick offers you some j-o-n-e-s, you ain't gonna take none?"

✦✦✦

"Well . . . I mean . . . if somebody wants to *give* me some j-o-n-e-s . . ."

So I was saying that I would welcome donations; but the truth was I knew as much about j-o-n-e-s as I knew about p-l-u-t-o-n-i-u-m. My neighborhood had signs on sidewalks and walls that said with simple eloquence JONES IS GOOD; but most of the boys who penned this lyrical thought were just sharing a rumor. I had never pondered it much because, in a foolish upside-down way, I had always been interested only in a girl's face. A few weeks before, when a girl had passed by, Pee Wee had told me, "I'd love to see her legs way up in the air."

"You wanna see her parachute from something?" I had replied.

And now Pee Wee again was discussing aerial maneuvers, this time by Rosemary.

"Rosemary wanna give you some j-o-n-e-s," he said.

"Naturally," I said, "but I'm not gonna take it."

"You're *not?* How come?"

" 'Cause I'm gonna marry her and I want her to be a virgin."

"Well, Rosemary ain't *nobody's* virgin. *Everybody* got some of that j-o-n-e-s. Even Weird Harold got some underneath the Ninth Street bridge."

In anguished disbelief, I threw down the ball and ran to Rosemary's house. Because of my pain, my first question to her perhaps was less diplomatic than it could have been.

"You givin' everybody some j-o-n-e-s?"

"*What?*" she replied.

"Have you been givin' everybody some j-o-n-e-s?"

"I don't give j-o-n-e-s to *nobody*."

"You didn't give some to Weird Harold underneath the Ninth Street bridge?"

"I wouldn't give Weird Harold the right *time*, under a bridge or in a *balloon*."

"Okay, then, would you give *me* some j-o-n-e-s?"

"Are you *crazy?* My mother's home."

"Okay, then when can you give me some?"

She paused for a moment, mentally reviewing her schedule for distributing herself.

"On Saturday," she said.

"Saturday's good; I'm free. Where?"

"Here."

"*Here?* Your mother move *out?*"

"She goes to work."

"That's my kind of mother. A night job too might be nice."

For the rest of that week, I was a cockeyed Kinsey, doing more than a dozen man-in-the-street interviews about j-o-n-e-s. I was the Inquiring Pornographer, always trying not to reveal that j-o-n-e-s was f-u-z-z-y to me. My scholarship generally sounded like this:

"Man, have you ever had any j-o-n-e-s?"

++

"Oh, *yeah.*"

"Well, what's your favorite way of getting it?"

"The regular way."

"You mean . . . there's *irregular* ways too?"

"Yeah, but I like it the regular way."

"Well, who doesn't?"

Lacking the nerve to request a definition of the regular way, I now began to fear the embarrassment of removing my pants for Rosemary and then not knowing what to do next. I feared that she might be confused by my seeming to be undressing for a physical and might say, "You don't know how to *do* it?"

And I would reply, "Of course I do, but I forgot."

Not wanting to turn our Big Moment into a sex education class for me, I now went to a newsstand to find a men's magazine that had some pictures of people getting ready to do it; but magazines had no erotic instructions in those innocent days and the Kinsey Report had no illustrations.

When Saturday finally came, I approached Rosemary's house with still just a hunch about the nature of j-o-n-e-s. I had decided that it probably had something to do with sex, and I'd also decided I didn't want any. The sage who had written JONES IS GOOD, wise and poetic as he might have been, had nevertheless missed two points: Rosemary might get pregnant and I might get killed by her father; *or* Rosemary might not get pregnant and I might get killed by her father.

Warmed by these thoughts, I rang her doorbell.

"Hello, William," she said.

"Hello, Rosemary."

And now my heart began to pound, for I really loved this girl and thought of her as considerably more than just a package of J-o-n-e-s. Nervously, I went inside, she closed the door, and I didn't move too far from it. And then she did the loveliest thing: she pulled up her dress.

There it *was*, in all its glandular grandeur. Had I ever seen one of those things before, I probably would have seized this moment to run right out the door; but this was a new sight for me and a deeply fascinating one, like Grant's Tomb or the Grand Canyon.

So that's *it*, I thought as she held up her dress. *There it is. One way to get pregnant just has to be playing around with that.*

Uncertainly, I moved toward her, trying to follow my heart and not my hormones, and then I pulled down her dress to show that I came in peace and we merely rubbed against each other awhile.

"Oh, nuts," I suddenly said, backing away from her a bit. "You gotta excuse me, Rosemary."

"What do you mean? You didn't do nothin' wrong.

You didn't do nothin' right either, but we're just startin'."

"No, I mean I gotta leave."

"Why?"

"I just remembered that I gotta help my mother wash the floors."

"So what you're sayin' is you don't wanna do it."

"Sure I wanna do it, but on a day when I don't have the floors. Just lemme check with my mother and see when I'm free to do it."

For a couple of seconds, she was silent while she fixed me with a suspicious look. "You *sure* you like to do it, William?"

"Are you kidding, Rosemary? I been doing it since I was ten: it's always been my *hobby.* But you see, when I do it, I gotta do it for a long time, like five or six hours at least."

"When you gonna have that kind of time?"

"Well . . . Thanksgiving might be good."

"You won't have floors?"

"Or windows neither."

And so, I left my bewildered beloved, who was probably ready to take religious vows, and returned to the land of Pee Wee.

"You been over to Rosemary?" he said.

With a smile of sensuous satisfaction, I replied, "Well, I ain't been pitchin' for the Phillies. The Phillies don't give you any j-o-n-e-s."

"Yeah! Ain't that stuff *good?*"

"Good ain't the word."

The word was "unknown," but I wanted Pee Wee to handle my public relations for the private kind.

"Did you come?" he said.

"Man, I came and went," I said, not inaccurately.

"Right away?"

"No, not right away. You don't just come and go so fast. You gotta have a little romance."

"So tell me, how did you do it?"

"Pee Wee, if you don't *know*, I ain't gonna tell you. Go ask your mother."

"Hell, a *mother* don't know how to do it. *Come* on, Bill, *tell* me."

"Some things gotta be private," I said with a devilish smile as I turned and began to walk away. Moments later, however, something moved me to look back and cry to my poor ignorant friend:

"We did it the *regular* way."

4

SOMEBODY MOP THAT CHAPEL

Alas, Rosemary and I did not last. In spite of all we had in common—our both living in North Philadelphia, our both knowing Weird Harold, our both being students of j-o-n-e-s—we soon drifted apart and I decided to find another wife. I was thirteen years old and back in the singles' scene.

Because that singles' scene was a lower economic one, parties were held not in restaurants or hotels but in somebody's house. We moved the furniture back, replaced the bright white light bulb with a soft red one, and put on records that were hard black 78s. As breakable as my heart, these records lasted less than three minutes; and so, less than three minutes was all you had to conquer the girl in your arms with a kind of pre-rock and roll dancing that I call rock and rub.

+++

You enveloped the girl, hoping that she would fit neatly into the contours of your body, and then you slowly rocked her as if you were putting a baby to sleep, while you suffered the awful suspense of wondering if she was going to press you back before she saw that you were sweating and left you for Weird Harold's cousin, Goofy Rufus.

It was a trip to the moon if the girl gave you both a little pelvis *and* a little knee (no other parts were required) in what was called The Grind. The problem, however, in my inspiring a girl to do The Grind was that a 78 was over too soon for me to make all my moves. What I needed was *The Nutcracker Suite* on 33⅓. With some of those girls, it seemed that I would have to rock around the clock before I got a knee jerk going.

Every time I think of those parties, one particular song comes hauntingly back to me through the years: "Crying in the Chapel" by Sonny Till and the Orioles. I must have heard this song a hundred times when I was thirteen: that chapel was flooded with Sonny's tears, while I kept trying not to turn soggy with sweat. No song accompanied more grinding than "Crying in the Chapel," but they were misplaced grinds, for we could not have picked a less appropriate song for sex. When I finally happened to listen closely to its lyrics many years later, I realized that we had been grinding our way from Philadelphia to hell because these were the words that fanned our lust:

> *You saw me crying in the chapel.*
> *The tears I shed were tears of joy.*
> *And now I'm happy in the chapel*
> *Because I have found the Lord.*

Yes, grinding to "Crying in the Chapel" was precisely the same as pursuing j-o-n-e-s to "Ave Maria."

Still on the rebound from Rosemary, I continued to drift through those homey red-light districts of the North Philadelphia singles' scene, doing The Grind whenever I could, until I came to rest on Ruth. It happened in the house of a friend whose parents were deeply religious people and probably prayed to "Crying in the Chapel." That evening, they stood by and watched piously as about twenty-five of us potentially sinful postpubescents, fueled by no more than fruit punch, put on the 78s and danced. Desperately, I was seeking a woman who would make me forget Rosemary, perhaps merely by keeping her dress down.

And suddenly, there was Ruth, in whose thick and shining hair was a stunning big braid. How I loved that big braid: to me it was an under-appreciated erogenous zone, for I had almost no interest in breasts or legs when I was thirteen. I was a braid man, maybe the only one in Pennsylvania.

As I began to slow dance with Ruth, I was elated to find that this was the first time I had ever danced with a girl who didn't seem as though she wanted to relocate. Moreover, there was a wondrous sweetness in the heat that came to me from Ruth's body. I sometimes had slept with my brother and this was definitely better.

In dancing with Ruth, I did not pull her right in to me: I just made sure she knew in what direction I would be going, and often I knew it too. Every time she moved one of her feet, there was a good chance that the other would follow; we had that kind of style. Although our bodies were about four inches apart, we still felt the heat across the divide. There was only one flaw in the rapture we knew: we couldn't look at each other. While we danced, Ruth kept looking all over the room, as if following birds, and I did some bird-watching too. But perhaps eye contact would have broken the spell.

When the song was over, I finally looked at Ruth and thanked her; and then I reluctantly retreated to the boys and began to look around for another vacant girl. Moments later, the search was over, for Millie came by.

I was delighted to discover that she didn't believe in gaps. In fact, when I put my arm around her waist,

++

she sweetly responded by straddling my right thigh with both of her legs, and then she began to press me with her bosom too. Here was a girl who knew how to press a hundred and twenty pounds: as we danced in slow circles, with the music low and my temperature rising, she made herself a part of my chest, my legs, and my face.

For almost three minutes, my fever climbed; and then the record ended, Millie released me to recover, and I returned to the punch bowl. There I waited out two fast songs, impatiently wondering if I would ever be able to go to press again. At last, a slow song came on, but both Ruth and Millie were taken, so I had to settle for a girl named Barbara, who was less attractive than those two: she wore no braid in her hair and she had no message for my thigh.

"You look nice," I told her as we began to dance with a gap that I wished were bigger.

"You look nice too," she said.

"It's a nice party."

"It sure is. Nice."

At least she was able to keep up with me conversationally.

"You live in Philadelphia?" I said.

There were probably better questions I could have asked (few girls in the room had flown in from Cleveland), but she wasn't commanding my total attention.

"Yes," she said.

✦✦

"Nice city."

"Yeah, really nice."

Enchanting though all this talk was, I still managed to tear myself away from it, perhaps too abruptly: in the middle of the next song, I spun away from Barbara and grabbed Ruth, as if hopping on a passing trolley. Barbara must have sensed that something was wrong when I went off with Ruth, but she graciously threw no punch glass at me.

On this time around with Ruth, I decided to show her what Millie had taught me, so I pulled her closer, but she stopped me at the two-inch mark. I was disappointed, but I didn't jump ship as I'd just done with Barbara. I continued to dance, for I loved a challenge: I had to lower that gap.

When the next record, another slow one, came on, I asked Ruth to dance again with the look of a man at the Penn Relays. And when she didn't respond to my tender tugging, I took my 440 stride and brushed her thigh. Suddenly, she brushed back and the angels were singing the way they had sung when I'd gotten interwoven with Millie. Although I wasn't getting a full chest press from Ruth, getting thigh was a step in the right direction.

My ecstasy ended when a fast record came on and Ruth left me for a real dancer. This time, however, I bounced back from the punch bowl within seconds and I landed on Millie, singing to myself:

+++

The press is wonderful
The second time around.

And the lyrics were true: this time Millie pressed me as if she were making wine. It was there and then I knew that I wanted to spend the rest of my life at parties with Millie. My problem was, however, that I was intellectually drawn to Ruth as a candidate for being my wife. Would she understand if I brought along Millie too? I had stumbled upon one of life's ancient dilemmas: Did I want a home and a family or fifty years of good pressing?

As I danced with Millie and thought about Ruth, I was sweating the way I did when I played basketball; but sex was harder than basketball because I didn't know the rules for staying out of foul trouble. Millie and I were back in a full-court press, Sonny Till was still scattering tears around that chapel, and my hands were getting wet too. I wondered if Clark Gable ever got sweaty palms; and I wondered how he would have handled the trickle of sweat now making its way down my face. However, while thinking that I should have been dancing with a headband, I noted happily that Millie was sweating too. I wondered if there could be a graceful way to stop and wipe, or if some passing friend could casually blot me while saying hello, some friend who happened to have a sponge.

+++

Even worse than the sweat was the sound that our
faces made whenever they pulled apart: it sounded
like the removal of surgical tape. As I tried to sustain
some feeling of romance, I was torn by two urges,
both unacceptable: to wipe my own sweat and to
wipe Millie's. And yet it seemed to me that if you
truly loved this girl in your arms, you'd remove your
hand and take a few seconds to dry her off, either
with a handkerchief or your sleeve. Was there a way
to get dry to music without breaking the spell? And
was there a way to keep yourself from starting to
sweat again? Did Fred and Ginger ever go to a rosin
bag?

And so, I entered the teenage years flitting from girl
to girl and dampening them as I wondered which of
them would be my True Love. It was only on the
dance floor that I ever got a female in both my arms
(in the movies, I used just one and it quickly died), so
I worked as hard on my dancing as I did on my driving to the hoop because I didn't want my dancing to
look like my driving to the hoop. My teacher was an
older boy named Johnny Berg, who didn't know the
capital of the United States but knew the two major
fast dances. Anyone, even Weird Harold, could do a
slow dance: you just leaned on the girl and moved as
if you were leaving a crowded bus; but you needed

either Astaire or Johnny to teach you the Bop and the Strand.

In the Bop, you circled your stationary partner, trying to stay in orbit and not float off into space like a loose comet; and in the Strand, you strolled across the floor with your partner in your arms and then suddenly flung her away from you, took a few steps, and met her again, as if she were a well-thrown yo-yo. If properly done, the Strand was charming. If improperly done, it looked as if you had disposed of the girl as if she were a frilly banana peel.

My study of these dances took a new direction on the day that my father came home and found Johnny Berg embracing me in our living room.

"Bill," he solemnly said, "can you *explain* this?"

"Oh, sure," I replied. "First you walk a few steps and then you fling him away."

The following day, I changed teachers and began taking lessons with my mother. She was a natural for the Strand. She often felt inclined to throw me away.

5

IN TRAINING
FOR VAGRANCY

For a boy entering puberty, love can involve different combinations of the head, the heart, and the glands. The head and the glands, however, were inactive when I fell in love with Sarah McKinney because she had certain qualities that made her unique as one of my flames: she was twenty-five years old, she was married, and she was my teacher. The tall skinny boy named Bill Cosby with a zit on his face and zip in his pockets had as much chance of winning Sarah McKinney as he had of winning Sarah Vaughan.

But what a vision she was as she kept trying to put something into my head: a dark chocolate woman with high cheekbones, large lovely eyes, and ebony hair that was parted in the middle. And how my heart turned over when she said, "The capital of Finland is Helsinki." I wanted to carry her off to Helsinki, or at least to Harrisburg.

My feeling for this woman had a purity from Camelot. In my fantasies about her, I never dreamed of taking her to bed or having her throw me down and do something from the Kinsey Report: I simply dreamed of saying to her, *Mrs. McKinney, you are the most beautiful woman I have ever seen, and when I get older I would like to take you to dinner. Your husband can come too.*

Whenever I played ball in the school yard, I watched for Mrs. McKinney and waited for the moments when she spoke my name, when she smiled at me and said, "William, your pants are unzipped." No woman has ever turned my unzipped pants into such poetry; and no woman has ever given me an afternoon of such fundamental joy as Mrs. McKinney did when she and her husband took me to a major league baseball game.

It was hardly a triangle from Noel Coward, the three of us at the ballgame that day. As we sat in the sunshine, I couldn't help noticing the allure of Mrs. McKinney's glistening red lips; but they were not the place to put mine, which glistened with mustard. She was buying me as many hot dogs as I wanted and I wanted about seventeen, for this was the first time in my life that I had ever been able to eat without a limit. Where would I ever find another woman like this, who would stuff me senseless while I watched the Phillies lose?

That young man filling up with meat needed female financing because he never had any money. I couldn't even afford to take a girl for a trolley ride and win her the way that Judy Garland was won in *Meet Me in St. Louis.* All that *I* could sing was:

> *Meet me in North Philly, Millie,*
> *And lend me the fare.*

The trolley, however, did have a place when I fell in love with a girl named Doris Mann, who was in my junior high but not my classes. The trolley I took to this school, a half hour ride I could barely afford, passed Doris's house; and whenever it did, I felt the same tingle I had felt when passing Sarah McKinney in the school yard. You can see that, except for those rare moments when I was getting a full body press, I generally loved from afar.

A few weeks after I had started loving Doris Mann from afar, the incredible invitation came: she asked me if I wanted to walk her home.

"You *bet;* I'll get you there," I said, as if the odds had been against her making it alone.

As we walked toward her house on that golden day, I was still so fearful about the chance of being rejected that I kept expecting her to stop at some manhole and say, *This is far enough. Stay here and direct some traffic.* However, she let me go all the way to her house, a place where my friends had told me I should try for another kind of all the way. Unfortunately, all the way in the afternoon was too long a trip for me. Although the boys had breezily talked about getting to second and third base with girls, I doubted that even at midnight I'd be able to make more than a foul pop-up with Doris, in spite of how much I loved her and in spite of my competitive zeal. The best I ever did was the second time I walked her home, when I found the courage to give her a quick kiss, in which she decided not to participate.

Perhaps my problem was the state of my face. I had been trying to get to first base with Doris at the worst time in a young man's life, when his glands are erupting and so is his skin. Of course, Doris might have been inclined to dispose of me even if I hadn't been decorated by what are now called zits; but my dermatological heartbreak was unique, for I had my zits single file. I never had *zits:* I always had only *one.* And masking it was out of the question because all the skin medication sold in those days was for white skin; acne hadn't reached the Third World.

Even brown shoe polish would have done no good for my most memorable zit, the one at the end of my nose that lasted a week but seemed like a lifetime. In desperation, I covered it with a Band-Aid, hoping that people wouldn't notice it; but the people who weren't comatose did and they asked me what had happened.

"I got a bee sting," I told one friend, referring to one of the seven bees in North Philadelphia since Benjamin Franklin had died.

"I got a little scratch shaving," I told another, revealing myself to be the first man in history who didn't know the location of his beard.

"I got it diving for a loose ball," I told a third, who must have suspected that something was loose besides that ball.

At last, I removed the Band-Aid, just in time for people to be distracted from the zit by another one on the bridge of my nose. How I envied the Lone Ranger and the Phantom of the Opera.

No matter how poor you were or how badly you danced or how many zits adorned your face, there was still one way to go after girls that required only the ability to stand in one place for two or three hours without realizing that nothing was happening. Because there were no discos in Philadelphia in those days, my teenage friends and I spent many truly empty evenings just standing in front of a drugstore and watching girls go by, dreaming of using the Trojans that we had bought in that drugstore years ago and that were making permanent rings in our wallets.

"I *got* it last week," one of our budding vagrants would say with a triumphant smile.

Got *what?* I wondered. *Athlete's foot?* The guy had never left the corner. Had he gotten it in the drugstore when we weren't looking?

"*I* could have gotten it," I replied, "but I didn't happen to be in the mood."

"Oh, yeah? You need a *woman* to get it, you know."

"You think I don't know that?"

"Well, *I* got it," he said, "and it was great."

"Soon as I have a free minute, I'm gonna get it too," I said. "I may very well be in the mood this week."

"Are you kiddin', Cosby? You don't even know what it *looks* like."

"Man, now you've gone too far! You want me to *tell* you what it looks like?"

"How do I know you won't be describin' your *mother?*"

"'Cause a mother is different."

"Now I *know* you don't know nothin'. They're all exactly the *same.*"

"And that's why all I'm gonna have to find is *one,*" I said.

The quality of the jive on that corner reached the level of the United Nations, for our imaginations had to fill endless stretches of time in which our lives had

all the drama of a crossing guard's. As we waited
there night after night, we knew that the girls simply
had to appear. We had never known where they went
in the daytime while we were playing six hours of
basketball; and so, if they were in some kind of
hibernation by day, it was logical to think they'd
come out at night, like the Dracula some of them re-
sembled. And eventually, they did: to go to the drugstore for their mothers to get a prescription, a
hairnet, or a picture of Mickey Rooney's latest wife.

Standing there between that drugstore and the bus
stop for hours every night, we seven or eight young
men were classic American dreamers. Being bonded
to other lustful liars gave us the confidence that each
of us lacked alone, no matter how many times we
claimed to have gotten it. The poignant truth was that
most of us were as sexually active as the Vatican
Boys' Choir.

We were fifteen and sixteen, almost the age of the
men who were fighting in Korea, and we were after
so little. All we wanted was the *scent* of a girl. We had
finished a day of basketball and then we had bathed
and eaten dinner and maybe even bathed again, all to
prepare for an evening of what looked like training to
be bus inspectors.

"Why aren't those boys doing something worthwhile?" one passing adult would say to another.

But nothing was more worthwhile than hanging

out, for this was our pre-mating ritual—*very* pre-, a ritual that has passed into American folklore, like the house call and the nongiggling newscaster. Young men no longer stand at drugstores and make plaintive cries to young women in this age of the equal female; but what memories I have of those boyhood evenings at a bus stop named desire.

I remember the acceleration of my heart one night when a particular object of my fancy came by. She had already rejected every other guy, but I still dreamed she would fall for me; I dreamed that maybe her weakness was a man with a zit on the bridge of his nose. She was aloof and elusive, this beauty, a girl who walked as erectly as a Marine, was always well dressed, and never went to parties because at parties you met guys like us. The problem was that she would have to fall for me without my encouragement because whenever I saw her, I was transfixed, afraid to make a move or utter a word. Sometimes one of the guys would walk one of the girls into the drugstore, but I never had the nerve to approach this princess. What could I have said?

Does your mother have gas again?

Guess how many buses stop here every hour.

Did you like the way World War II came out?

Like that famous tree in the forest without people, when Cosby fell for a girl, did he make any sound?

♥

On certain nights, we drugstore dreamers remained at our watch so long that our parents felt we must have been misbehaving.

"What were you *doing* till after midnight?" my father said early one morning when I returned from another plunge into unrequited love.

"Nothing," I replied.

"Well, tonight you can do it in the house."

"But it's better to do nothing *outdoors*. You see, a lot of my friends also like to do nothing and we do it *together*."

"Then have 'em come here."

"It's not the same kind of nothing."

"Exactly what kind of nothing do you do outdoors?"

"We stand at the bus stop."

"And do what? Make change?"

"No, we just watch the traffic."

"Okay, suppose I gave you a job and paid you two bucks an hour to stand on that corner and just watch people get on and off the bus. You wouldn't stand there an hour."

"I would if I could have my *friends* with me."

"But they wouldn't be with you because they have a little mental problem. They're terrified of work."

"Dad, you don't understand. What I'm looking for on that corner is the woman of my life."

+++

"You don't know any girls who walk around any-place else? You gotta meet buses?"

"I go to an all-boys' school and it's got no girls for me to carry their books. I always thought I could get a girl from the way I play basketball, but they never watch me play because they never come out in the daytime. Dad, do *you* know where girls go in the day-time?"

He frowned and was silent for a few seconds.

"Maybe they leave Philadelphia," he said.

"That's why I'm watching the buses."

Night after night, year after year, I looked for a girl with whom I could go steady. From time to time, on a Friday or Saturday night, I left bus inspecting to look for her at a party, which was usually held in some-body's basement. In one corner of the room, there was always a phonograph; and in the center of the room, there was a punch bowl, peanuts, and pink and white mints that tasted like something that should have been unclogging a drain. The air was so full of cigarette smoke that after a while the hostess's par-ents went outside so they could continue breathing, leaving us young lovers to grope for each other with watery eyes to the strains of "Crying in the Chapel."

It was in those basements that I tried to squeeze girls as if they were melons to see which ones might be ripe for going steady with me. Sometimes I man-aged to lure one of them outside to sit with me in a car for a little kissing and rubbing; most of the other girls I managed to lure away from the crowd just sat there like statues, hoping that this moment would pass and they could get on with their lives.

For these statuesque girls, every boy knew precisely the physical therapy that was needed, the quintessential behavior modifier.

"You know what *she* needs," one of us would say.

"Absolutely," another would reply. "It would straighten her out."

The problem was that this profound psychological insight was never translated into field work, for none of us had the technique to straighten a girl out, in either the horizontal or emotional sense. But how certain we were that one would lead to the other; in fact, I used to dream of running a special kind of social service agency. A girl would call me and say, "Hello, Bill, this is Ella and I need help."

"Yes, Ella," I would say. "How can I be of service?"

"Well, I've been feeling so unresponsive lately. My hormones are just lying there."

"Oh, not good, not good; they're supposed to be moving."

"Bill, I've heard you know what I need."

"I'm blessed with that knowledge, yes."

"What time can you come to my house?"

"Well, let's see," I would tell her in a tender yet professional tone. "From eight to nine there's a girl in

+++

Germantown I have to save . . . and there's another in Girard who requested saving before dinner . . . but my schedule *is* flexible. Are your parents going to be home tonight?"

"Yes, but not on Saturday."

"Good, I'll be there. Just try to hold on till Saturday. Take some cold showers and go to church—but stay away from 'Crying in the Chapel.'"

And then the fantasy ended and again I was just a wistful boy with a good jump shot and bad skin, a boy still waiting for public transportation to deliver his private dream.

6

A FLING ON THE TRACK

During my last year of high school, I fell in love so hard with a girl that it made my love for Sarah McKinney seem like a stupid infatuation with a teacher. Charlene Gibson was the Real Thing and she would be Mrs. Charlene Cosby, serving me hot dogs and watching me drive to the hoop and giving me the full-court press for the rest of my life.

In tribute to our great love, I was moved to give Charlene something to wear. A Temple T-shirt didn't seem quite right and neither did my Truman button. What Charlene needed was a piece of jewelry; and I was able to find the perfect one, an elegant pin, in my mother's dresser drawer.

Ten days after I had made this grand presentation, Charlene dumped me; but, sentimentalist that she

+++

was, she kept the pin. When I confessed my dark deed to my mother, she didn't throw a brick at me, she merely wanted to have the pin back, a request that I felt was not unreasonable since I had stolen it. Moreover, retrieving the pin was important to *me*, but for a romantic reason: I wanted to punish Charlene. Paying back the person with whom you have recently been in love is one of life's most precious moments.

"I want that pin back," I said to Charlene on the phone.

"I can't do that," she replied.

"Why not?"

"Because I lost it."

"You *lost* it?"

"That's what I just said."

"How could you *lose* it?"

"Easy. First I had it, then I didn't."

And so, I went to her house, where her mother said she wasn't home. Nervously I told her mother why I needed the pin returned and she understood without saying I had done anything wrong. Of course, she didn't have the world's sharpest judgment because she still thought I was a wonderful person. In fact, *all* the mothers of the girls who rejected me thought I was a wonderful person; I would have made a fine father to those girls.

"Mrs. Gibson," I said, "Charlene told me she lost

the pin. I'm not saying I don't believe her, but I don't."

"Just one minute, William," she said, and she turned and went upstairs. Moments later, she returned with the pin. And then I went home and waited for the satisfaction of Charlene calling me to say:

How dare you go to my house and ask my mother for that pin!

But no call from her came.

Probably because she's ashamed of lying to me, I told myself; *but maybe because she truly likes me and wants to keep the pin for that reason.*

I was convincing myself that Charlene wanted to have an elegant token of me and that now I should call *her* to rekindle this wondrous love-hate relationship, for Charlene and I had been meant for each other: she was a liar and I was a thief. Two such people, who had been so deeply in love, should have had a chance to keep torturing each other. We once had kissed for almost three hours, inhaling each other and talking about how many children we should have. True, she was the kind of girl who might be having children by other men too, but there was still a softness about her I liked, a softness that matched the one in my head. We had been too close for our relationship to end with her dumping me. We had to get back together so I could dump *her*.

+++

All these thoughts went through my head as I sat with my hand on the phone, wanting to get into a fight with Charlene for old times' sake. Shakespeare said that the lunatic and the lover are the same, but he was wrong: the lunatic has more sense than the man who wanted to call Charlene so that he could hang up on her. However, I had to be very careful to keep her from hanging up on *me* or else she would have been two ahead of me, with no overtime to play.

Finally, after the kind of reasoning that made Napoleon invade Russia, I picked up the phone.

"Hello, Charlene," I said, at least beginning well by getting her name right.

"Yes," she coldly replied, neatly falling into my trap.

"I think you owe me an apology."

"Oh, is that what you think?"

"It certainly is."

Note how cleverly I was preparing her for the kill.

"So that's the way you feel?" I said. "That no apology is necessary?"

"That's the way I feel; I just said it. You have some problem with English?"

"No, I'm just checking to see if you really want to keep the reputation of being a dishonest person and lying about having something that belonged to somebody else."

"You stole the pin from your mother and you're calling *me* dishonest?"

"But you didn't *know* I stole it. And it meant something special to me."

"I didn't *ask* you to give it to me," she said.

"But you *lied* about losing it."

"No, I didn't. I didn't know where it was."

"Your mother went right upstairs and found it."

"Just the way *you* found it in your mother's drawer."

My appetite for humiliation was clearly boundless as I pressed on in a conversation that revealed new dimensions in male dumbness.

"Put your mother on the phone," I said.

"Put *your* mother on the phone," she said, "and I'll ask her how it feels to have a crazy son."

"Crazy, huh? It just so happens that I was crazy in love with you. Have you already forgotten our plans to have children?"

"Well, start without me. I'm definitely not having them if they're yours."

"And that's just fine with me."

"Me too."

"Look, Charlene . . . I don't think we should end this by being angry with each other."

"Yeah, I guess not."

"I know that you're in love with someone else this week and I wish you the best."

+-+

"Coming from you, that means nothing to me."

"Look, Charlene, I think we should end this by being friends. I think we should end it so . . . well, so if you ever want to call me and ask me a question, like how to break a zone defense or something, I'll be happy to give you the answer."

Now note how cleverly I was luring her into a position where I could dump her last and make her feel sorry she had ever known me, a sentiment she already may have felt.

"I don't think I'll be calling you," she said.

"So that's the way you feel?"

"Why do I have to tell you everything twice? I think I've told you enough."

And then she hung up. She hadn't even said good-bye—once.

Should I call her back to slam her with my own good-bye? I asked myself.

No, I decided. I would find the revenge that she deserved for messing around with my heart, the only part of my body that I could never get into shape.

The revenge I devised had a simple splendor: I would find a girl who was prettier than Charlene, entice her into a relationship, and then flaunt this relationship to Charlene, who would promptly jump off a cliff. And so, with both the dedication and the mental balance of Captain Ahab chasing Moby Dick, I began my great hunt. The following day, I began pursuing a gorgeous girl I'll call Artemis, after the Greek Goddess of Virginity. For many months, boys had been throwing themselves at Artemis like tacklers trying to bring down Jim Brown. Nonetheless, on this day, I summoned the courage to approach her and say, "Hi, I'm Bill Cosby and I was wondering if you're going to John Thomas's party on Friday night."

She looked at me silently for a moment, but I knew that she knew who I was because I had played varsity basketball on nights when the girls had come out of hiding.

"No, I'm not going," she said.

And suddenly I feared that her refusal to go with me would get back to Charlene and make her heart sing.

"But we've been talking about going, haven't we?" said one of several girls who made up Artemis' entourage.

Fixing me with a cool look, she said, "What time's the party?"

"Eight o'clock," I replied.

"Okay, I'll go with you."

"Yeah, we'll go with you," said one of her friends.

"Right, we'll go," said a third.

"Could I talk to you alone for a minute?" I said to Artemis.

"I guess so," she said, clearly falling for me.

+++

Taking her hand, I led her away from the entourage and said, "Look, I want to go to the party with *you*, not a field hockey team."

"They're my friends."

"And I'm glad you have them. But can't you give them a night off and go just with *me?*"

"I thought you were going steady with Charlene."

"Yeah, I was, but *she* wasn't, so I released her. And a lucky thing too 'cause it made room for you. Listen, you want to come and watch track practice this afternoon?"

"Not really."

"I do the high jump."

"I'm sure you do."

"And I'll be jumping just for you."

"The way you jumped for Charlene?"

"Charlene was just a high hurdle compared to you."

And not sounding like an idiot was a high hurdle for me too, but this divine female was heady stuff.

"Okay, then," she said, "you'll pick me up on Friday around eight?"

"You bet," I said, wondering how I was going to pick her up in a trolley.

When Friday came, however, I was able to pick her up in a car driven by my friend Ed Ford, who'd agreed to double date because he couldn't believe that Artemis had fallen off her pedestal and into the depths occupied by me.

✦✦✦

"I still don't see her going with *you,*" said Ed as we drove to her house. "Maybe she's gonna become a nun and has to do some kinda suffering."

"You just don't understand women," I said. "She *knows* I'm using her to pay back Charlene, and she's doing it 'cause women hate each other. But the funny thing is, I'm also falling in love with her."

"And when she dumps you, who you gonna use to punish *her?*" said Ed. "Lena Horne? Man, you're over your head in beauty."

But he was wrong: I had *lost* my head in beauty, so the Friday party became a blend of revenge and desire for me. A few minutes after Artemis and I had arrived, while I was busy parading her like a poodle going for Best in Show, Charlene came in—and suddenly, my future and past were together in one room. Charlene saw me with Artemis, of course, and I was delighted that her suffering had begun. Putting my face close to Artemis' face, I broke into laughter, as if she had just said something hilarious.

"You feelin' okay?" she said.

"Never better," I told her, still laughing.

"You been hittin' that high bar a lot?"

"I love it when you talk like that."

A few seconds later, seeing Charlene move to the punch bowl, I said to Artemis, "Will you excuse me for a moment?"

"For as long as you want," she replied.

I turned and walked over to Charlene, casually saying, "Why, Charlene Gibson, I *thought* it was you. What're *you* doing here?"

"Making a big mistake," she said. "Artemis and *you?* Since when did she start doing social work with thieves?"

"Glad you're having fun, Charlene."

"What're you gonna steal for *her?* Your mother's *watch?*"

"Have some pink and white mints. They'll really clear your head."

"I know you, Bill Cosby. You're just rentin' that girl to make me feel bad. I thought you wanted to be friends."

"Well, I did," I said, suddenly wishing that I had chosen a more gracious revenge.

"I thought you wanted me to be able to ask you questions."

"Well . . . yeah."

"Okay, here's one: Are you ever gonna grow up?"

It was a simple true-false question, the kind on which I usually guessed, and so I took a guess now: "I certainly am."

Often through the years, I have thought of Charlene's question; and I now know the answer is that no man ever grows up in the eyes of a woman— or ever grows familiar with the rules for dealing with her. Sigmund Freud once said, "What do women want?" The only thing I have learned in fifty-two years is that women want men to stop asking dumb questions like that.

My ignorance of women, however, still has not kept me from being certain that they are impressed by athletic daring, that a female grows weak from watching a male grow strong on the field of sport. It has always been my medieval belief that the closer a man comes to killing himself, the more romantic he is.

I was almost suicidally romantic at a track meet in my freshman year at Temple, when a friend of mine brought a blind date for me on what was really a scouting trip. A tall, pretty girl named Lori Ruddy, she had told my friend that she would not go out with me at night if she didn't like the way I looked on the track. In other words, I was having a sweaty audition for this girl, who would give me the kind of scoring you didn't get in the Penn Relays. ("Charming behind, but a rather stupid face.") Once again, I was involved with my old friend, humiliation.

The first event of that track meet was the high jump, a thrill that Artemis had decided to skip in favor of washing her hair. With Lori now watching me, I jumped as if I were in the Olympics, but I came in third behind two men who used no sexual inspiration, just better legs.

✦✦

"How did you do?" said Lori right after the announcement that I had finished third.

"I came in third," I said.

"You didn't win?"

"No, if I'd won, I wouldn't be third."

She had a feeling for sport that was roughly equivalent to Mahatma Gandhi's.

"I see," she said. "Is there anything you can do better?"

"Well, I do the broad jump next."

"And you won't be running into the bar. So do you think you can win that?"

"If there's no bar, absolutely. But remember: it's not whether you win or lose, it's how you play the game."

"If you played it better," she said, "you'd win."

A few minutes later, I threw myself into the broad jump as if I were leaving a burning ship, and this time I managed to come in second.

"Well, how did you do at *that?*" she said.

"I came in second," I replied.

"Only second? I thought you were going to win."

"I guess I needed a better game plan."

"What do you do next?"

"Take a shower. I'll tell you how it comes out."

"You mean there's nothing else you can do out here?"

"Well, the high jump and broad jump are two very

—" And suddenly I remembered having heard that Temple had an opening in the hammer throw because its man was sick. "Yes, there *is:* I'll be in the hammer throw."

"You throw a *hammer?* At *what?*"

She had made it sound like a competition for cranky carpenters.

"Come to the other field with me and you'll see.."

"If I had a hammer . . ." she started to sing as we walked.

"It's not that kind of hammer," I said. "It's a big steel ball."

"Then why do they call it a hammer?"

"*I* don't know. They made a mistake."

And the second mistake, of course, had been mine: to think I could win a woman at an event that both of us were about to learn.

At the hammer throw area, where I turned out to be Temple's only entry against the University of Pittsburgh, there was a three-sided cage about twelve feet high, like the kind used for batting practice; and in front of it was a big circle in which the thrower would spin before he flung a sixteen-pound steel ball attached to a short wire. After taking my name, the judge moved to one side of the cage, while Lori moved to the other.

"Temple will throw first," he said. "Mr. Cosby."

This order of competition was indeed bad luck for

Temple because its entry was surely the first virgin hammer thrower in collegiate history. I had been hoping to watch the Pittsburgh man to see how it was done. All I now knew for certain was that, in throwing a hammer, it was possible to achieve both a separated shoulder and a hernia. Nevertheless, inspired again by Lori's face, I picked up the steel ball and started to twirl it in great circles, quickly gaining a splendid momentum and losing all sense of direction. Around and around I spun, drunk with centrifugal force, until I finally released the ball just before it lifted me into orbit. It slammed into the cage as if I were launching an attack on the stadium.

Lori and the judge looked shaken, but the Pitt man smiled, for he knew he would have no trouble beating a throw that had gone a negative distance. Sheepishly leaving the circle, I wondered if the judge would now announce, *Temple: minus twenty feet.* I also wondered what effect my reverse throw was having on Lori's questioning heart. Was there a chance that she was feeling a certain elation from having just missed an offbeat death? And I was also struck by the thought that I could have killed the judge or the man from Pitt. If the man from Pitt had taken my shot, I might have been declared the winner by default and impressed Lori at last.

Did you win? she would have asked me.

It was a tie, I would have said. *My opponent is dead,*

but the judge still feels that he has done as well as I did.

In a song from *A Chorus Line* called "What I Did for Love," a dancer movingly tells how far a man will follow his heart. Although I hadn't been in love with Lori, I still went to the brink of manslaughter for her. I shudder to think how much further love might have driven me. I might have put a javelin through the dean.

7

JUST BABY AND ME AND COLTRANE MAKES THREE

In my sophomore year at Temple, where I was majoring in physical education, I came across a girl named Denise, who was so beautiful that Artemis would have been one of her ugly friends; and she was highly intelligent too. In fact, she had been able to start college at fifteen, the age at which some of my friends were making tentative starts in high school.

Maybe at last this is the one, I thought on a morning when Denise again passed me on the campus. *Maybe all the others have just been spring training for me. Maybe it's finally good-bye to my Grapefruit League.*

"Forget her," said my friend Roy after I had dreamed aloud to him. "That girl is a stiff."

"Probably because nobody has ever approached her the right way," I said.

✦✦

"The right way is with an oil can. I tell you, Bill, the girl's a *stiff.*"

"Look, I'm majoring in physical education, so I happen to know what to do when somebody's stiff."

"You gonna tell her to take a few laps?"

"I'm also studying psychology. I understand the human mind."

"The human mind, okay, but what about women?"

In spite of Roy's doubts, I accepted the challenge of this intimidating beauty and I introduced myself.

"Hi, there," I said, intercepting her at the library. "I'm Bill Cosby. I've seen you around the campus 'cause I'm on it a lot 'cause I go here too."

Another smooth opening by the most romantic tongue since Cyrano.

"Hello, I'm Denise Carter."

"What's your major?" I said, falling back on the stalest campus question of all. The zenith of my conversation seemed to have been my name.

"English," she replied.

"Mine's phys ed, but I know a lot of English too. You like music?"

"I love it."

"Well, John Coltrane's playing at the Showboat. Would you like to go?"

"Where is it docked?"

"It's not a boat, it's a club."

"John Coldtrain?"

+++

"Yes, isn't that something?"

"Who *is* he?"

Ignorance of John Coltrane was similar to thinking that Babe Ruth was a burlesque queen, but I let it pass without a howl, for I was suddenly stirred by the idea of teaching something important to this rare blend of beauty and brains. She would be my Liza Doolittle and I would be her Professor Higgins.

"But you do like music," I said.

"Oh, I love music," she replied. "Especially Wagner."

Wagner . . . Wagner . . . There was a Harry Wagner who played forward for Villanova, but I didn't think he blew anything but layups. I decided not to ask her where this Wagner cat was playing, a question that would not have helped me establish myself as the dominant mind in this relationship.

Three nights later, with my entire portfolio represented by the fourteen dollars in my pocket, I walked into the Showboat with Denise to hear a genius of jazz. As John Coltrane began a sublime improvisation that would last for more than ten minutes, I took off with him; but when I glanced back, I saw Denise looking like someone who was waiting for a bus. Note after note was sending me skyward, but she was stuck on the ground.

"Isn't this the greatest stuff you've ever heard?" I said. "I mean, the man is just too much."

+++

"Well, to be honest," she said, "it's not really my kind of music."

"But . . . how can that *be?*" I wondered if she had some kind of rare ear disease.

"Very simply. Liking this music is a matter of taste."

"Yes, I *agree.* If you have taste, you like it."

She replied just by rolling her eyes and I fell silent too, for I was stunned. How could I marry a girl who didn't dig John Coltrane? I would come home from a hard day of whatever I was doing with phys ed, put on a Coltrane record, and she would say, "Can't you put on some Wagner?"

And I would say, "I'm fresh out of Wagner. How about some Bud Powell?"

"There are no musicians named Bud," she'd reply.

At the end of Coltrane's performance, I drove Denise home in a car I had borrowed for what should have been a magnificent evening.

"I'm afraid that your Mr. Coltrane has problems within himself," she said as we rode.

"You better explain that," I said, hoping she wouldn't.

"Well, he's punishing his audience by playing out his anger."

"Denise, *you're* the only one who felt punished."

"No, he's a very angry man and that isn't good."

"Look, don't you have angry men in classical music?" I said, and then I reached for the only classical reference I knew: "I hear Beethoven was in a rotten mood for thirty years."

And my own mood wasn't sunshiny either. It was maddening for a man when a woman couldn't tune to his wavelength. Was this a preview of my married life? Trying to explain obvious greatness to a foreign sex?

"Beethoven didn't write music that sounded like a train wreck," she said.

"A *train* wreck? That sounded like a *train* wreck to you? I guess you haven't been in too many train wrecks lately. You ever hear a wrecked train play 'Autumn Leaves'?" I paused to try to calm myself. "Denise, I hate to say this, but you're really square."

In spite of my anger, I enjoyed the thought that I had moved to a higher level of fighting with women. I was fighting now about art instead of my mother's stolen jewelry.

"I don't think we should talk about aesthetics any more," she said.

I was inclined to agree, primarily because I didn't know what aesthetics was; but then I heard myself say, "No, I think we *should.* I'll teach you about Mr. Coltrane and you can teach me about Mr. Wagner."

"I'd rather skip the Coltrane lessons; he gave me a headache. I've heard enough."

+++

"So. You think the Owls can go all the way this year?"

"All the way to what?"

A few minutes later, after some awkward talk about football, we reached her house, where I parked the car and said, "Denise . . . may I come in for a while?"

"Yes," she said with a shining face that revealed none of the fog beneath it.

As I walked into the house with her, I began feeling optimistic again. I remembered that Professor Higgins had needed more than just a couple of hours to renovate Liza Doolittle's mind.

"This is Bill Crosby," said Denise to her mother and father.

"A fine musical name," her father said.

Just like John Cold Rain.

Her parents then left and Denise and I sat down on the sofa, together but apart. I still was strongly attracted to her—whenever she wasn't talking.

"You go to many parties?" I said.

"Parties aren't important to me," she said. "Except political parties, of course."

"I don't go to those too often. Is there any dancing at them?"

She laughed and I smiled modestly. I always did have a gift for amusing women.

"You like to dance?" I asked her.

"Well . . . not really."

"You know how?"

"I'm afraid not."

"You want to learn?"

"No, I can't say I'm interested."

And so, here was a woman who went to no parties unless they had politicians, who couldn't dance or see a reason to learn, and who was moved by John Coltrane to picture a casualty list. Why was I still here? For the simple reason that a relationship between a man and a woman makes no sense.

"How'd you like to come and see a football game?" I said.

"Okay," she replied.

I knew I would finally get one right.

"You're majoring in physical education?" she said, as if inquiring about an accident.

"Yes, but I'm also thinking of being a behavioral scientist. And maybe win the Nobel prize for discovering why women hate jazz."

She smiled, but her heart wasn't in it, only those lovely lips.

"Are you going to teach?" she said.

"Probably. In the lower economic area."

"I could never marry a teacher."

"Why?" I said, also wondering why I was sitting with this woman instead of doing something more pleasant, like donating my body to a medical school.

+++

"Because they don't make enough money."

"But it's still a good living."

"For one person maybe; but I don't think I could live on a school teacher's salary. I want a big house and I want someone to clean it."

"Well, how about *you*—once in a while, I mean . . . every month or two."

"It's getting late, Bill. I've had a lovely evening."

When? I wanted to say. *Why didn't you take me along?*

"I could teach at a very fine school," I said, slowly getting up. "And tutor rich kids on the side. And take bets at night—but just in the good neighborhoods."

She smiled and my heart turned over again when she said, "You *are* an amusing man. Maybe I'll come and watch you play football."

"That isn't always funny," I said. "But yes, please come and watch."

"When does the season begin?"

"Three weeks ago."

"Did you win yet?"

Did you win? I had heard this question from a woman before and I was not happy to hear it again. The one thing I did not want to do in my failures with women was repeat myself. Let her watch football with Weird Harold and talk about all the Wagner records she could buy with the money he made as an orthodontist.

✦✦✦

In spite of these melancholy thoughts, as I drove away from her house, I knew that I still desired her; and I wondered if there could be room in our relationship for her hatred of my music, my dancing, and my job. How happy could she be at the PTA Dixieland Ball?

Men and women are different, I decided, a difference more profound than just the way that women looked or disappeared during the day. Women, I decided, are not just men who can have babies. How would I be able to spend a lifetime with such aliens?

When I reached my house, I went inside and at once sought comfort in a recording of "My Foolish Heart" by John Coltrane. For several minutes, his saxophone soared, the sweetest punishment I knew; and when its flight was over, I sat alone in my bedroom and pondered my future as one of the sexes. Suddenly, I saw myself winning a gold medal for the Olympic high jump. I saw myself proudly at attention on the winners' center step, while the stadium was filled by the sounds of "The Star-Spangled Banner."

And then Denise walked over to the step, looked up at me, and said, "I thought they only used that song to start Phillies games."

+++

8

Salvation Called Camille

Not long after my memorable evening of talking in a foreign tongue to Denise, I revealed a flair for insecurity by dropping out of Temple to become a stand-up comedian. I began to perform at little nightclubs all along the East Coast, trying to be as funny as women had found me when I pursued them. The day I reached Washington, a friend named George Green asked me if I wanted to go out with a beautiful nineteen-year-old student from the University of Maryland named Camille Hanks, whose family lived in the fashionable suburb of Silver Springs.

"She's a stunner, Bill," said George.

"And that just happens to be the woman I'm looking for," I said. "Tell her my own stunningness can't be seen by the naked eye, but it's there. Tell her I'm a great dancer, I have a great outside shot, and I'm never going to be a teacher."

"Her father is a research chemist."

"Tell her that's always been my hobby: researching chemistry. A really good-looking woman, eh?"

"More than good-looking, Bill; she has *class*. Come to think of it, I wonder why she'd want to go out with *you*."

He had wondered correctly: Camille Hanks considered the idea and decided that I should start the date without her. On her list of ideal men, a struggling comic did not appear. He was on a different list, one that included parolees, lion tamers, and freelance chimney sweeps.

A few days later, however, George asked me if I wanted to come to a bowling class that he attended with Camille; and I accepted, for I saw a chance to win her in person and make her forget that she would never be able to tell our children what their father did for a living.

That evening at the bowling class, where Camille didn't know my name for a while, I improvised some comedy bits, inspired by the class having more people than most of the clubs where I worked. When I was finally introduced to her, she realized that she had already been enjoying me—but not nearly so much as I had been enjoying just the sight of her. In that Washington bowling alley, love at first sight became more than just another cliché for me; and I suddenly knew that, no matter how hard I had pursued those other girls, I had never been in love, just in like or in lust.

"Would you like to go out one night and hear some music with me?" I said to Camille.

"Yes, that would be nice," she replied. "Do you have any particular concert in mind?"

"Well, the New York Philharmonic doesn't seem to be in town, which is a bad break, so how about John Coltrane?"

He had followed me to Washington, daring me to bring him another woman.

"John Coltrane?" said Camille, looking as if I'd just mentioned a leader of the IRA.

Why, I wondered, did I always tie my heart to a saxophone? I saw myself at sixty-five, wandering through bus terminals and asking women in shawls, "Wanna come hear some Coltrane, honey?"

The following night, Camille went out with me and spent three hours trying to fly with John Coltrane. The Cosby College of Cool had a willing student at last, and one whose beauty matched the sounds that had me spellbound. The big question now was: Could a woman be laughed into love? I thought about the great lovers of history: Romeo, Casanova, Napoleon, and Loose Leroy Simms. They were pretty serious cats and they did better with women than Oliver Hardy and Fibber McGee. I wondered if women ever laughed when they were making love. Mrs. Weird Harold perhaps, but Jane Russell never cracked a smile when Billy the Kid was attending to her. And now *this* Billy the Kid was going for the greatest prize of his life with material that had never worked.

As a reward to Camille for spending an evening at Cosby College, I invited her to see a matinee of a movie with me the following Saturday. I was free only in the afternoon because on Friday and Saturday nights I was busy making strangers laugh. When she accepted my invitation, I felt as though I had just run a four-minute mile. Was this elegant woman feeling for me what I was feeling for her? Should I try to help things along by stealing for her my mother's brooch?

That Saturday, as we took our seats in the movie house, my mind was reeling with options. I knew there was no possibility of my touching Camille's breasts (I'd be lucky if she'd let me do that after we were married), but I wondered if I should try to make contact with something more acceptable, like her knee. I had never felt a woman's knee and I wondered how erotic it was to be palming that particular bone. Dr. Kinsey never spoke about knees, no one dove into the hay after Jane Russell's, and no one on the corner had ever said, "Man, tonight I'm gonna get me some k-n-e-e."

Perhaps I should try for something out in the open, like her hand. My right hand was fast enough to steal a moving basketball, so it would have no trouble trapping Camille's and filling it with sweat. However, during other dates in theaters, I had put my hand on a female's and instantly been called for a foul. Except for that body press from Millie, which had clearly been nothing personal, I had never been able to get past the starting blocks of sex. A man who dreamed of nookie, I couldn't even get knuckle.

When the movie began and I felt emboldened by the darkness, I considered casually slipping my arm across the back of Camille's seat, as if checking for termites and ticks, and then letting the arm gently drape itself across her right shoulder; but there were two dangers in making this move. The first was that Camille could turn to me and tenderly say, "Remove that, please." And if she left the arm there, it might fall asleep, as it had done in theaters before. This movie was more than two hours long, so I'd be taking the romantic road to gangrene.

What I did take, however, was a third approach. A few minutes after the lights went low for a film called *The Apartment,* my arm was still awake but my head was asleep. All the late-night comedy work had left me too tired for love in the afternoon. On the other hand, going unconscious was probably a good move for me because it was the one state in which I wouldn't be able to say, "John Coltrane."

And so, there I sat, asleep beside the girl of my dreams, a girl from the horsey set beside a boy from the drugstore drones.

A tap on my shoulder brought me partially back to life.

"Is it my stop?" I mumbled.

"Your stop?" said Camille.

"Oh, yeah—it's a *movie.* Did I leave a wake-up call?"

"I would've let you sleep but you were snoring," she said with a smile that lit up the theater for me.

"Look, my going to sleep, it was nothing *personal . . .*"

"Oh, *I* know that; you're tired from all the nightclub work. We really didn't have to come here. We could've gone—"

"To bed?"

She laughed and said, "We'll stay in *this Apartment.*"

"Ssshhh!" said a man in front of us, who'd turned and then done a double take, for nothing on the screen was as attractive as Camille.

"You want to know what's happened?" she whispered.

"Thanks, I've got it."

I knew what had happened: I had fallen in love. I

wanted to be Camille's husband. I wondered if I would ever be able to tell her about it.

I now began a courtship that demonstrated that neither my car nor my mind was hitting on all cylinders. After my Washington club date, I went back to New York for a booking at the Bitter End, but my heart was still down south with Camille. Between shows, I often called her dorm at the University of Maryland and had to hear some young woman cry, "Phone for *Camille*. It's that guy again for *Camille* . . ."

"The goofy one?" said another voice.

"Yeah, Mister Laughs."

When Camille finally came to the phone, I said, "Hi, it's Bill."

"Oh, I thought it was Prince Philip," she said with a laugh.

"You free for lunch?"

"Well—"

"Great! I'll be down!"

"Again just for *lunch*? Bill, I'm studying abnormal psychology and we could put you on a *slide*."

"I love you too. Just don't transfer to another school before I get there."

Of all the people in New York who went to Maryland for lunch, I was probably the only one who took the New Jersey Turnpike in a '52 Chevrolet that was a pilot project for the lemon law. After I had finished performing at two or three o'clock in the morning, I would sleep until dawn and then dare the transmission to take me down to Maryland.

How intoxicating it was to be in love, to be making this mad trip south to Camille! My future was enchanting, my past a series of fading flops. How delicious it was to say all my good-byes . . .

Good-bye to Charlene, who had inspired me to become my mother's favorite burglar.

Good-bye to Doris, who had introduced me to the questionable pleasure of a unilateral kiss.

Good-bye to Denise, whose golden face had concealed a tin ear.

Good-bye to Sarah, who had chaperoned our date with her husband.

Good-bye to Ruth, who had turned out to be just a thigh that passed in the night.

Good-bye to Artemis, that gorgeous Goddess of Germantown, who had correctly decided that she was above me.

Good-bye to Rosemary, who had moved me to a new appreciation of washing the floor.

Good-bye to Lori, who had almost lost her head at the hammer throw because I had lost mine.

Good-bye to Millie, who for one sweet moment had made me forget that she was the school's official body presser.

And good-bye to . . . what was her name? The girl at that movie matinee, where desire had filled my heart and my bladder too.

My love life had left me with so many forgettable memories; but improved memories lay ahead with Camille, who promised infinitely more than a passing press or a sometime thigh or a loss of circulation. As I drove past Elizabeth (had I ever gone out with *her?*), I found myself singing:

> *Now I'm not crying in the chapel*
> *Or even frowning near a priest.*
> *Instead I'm smiling on the turnpike*
> *In spite of driving half the East.*

It was during one of those interstate lunches that I asked Camille to marry me.

"I'd love to marry you," she replied.

Suddenly I knew that I was one of God's favorites. And imagine my shock when one of God's favorites was rejected by two of Camille's parents, who believed that stand-up comedians were an early link in the chain of evolution. What heartbreaking irony! In all my years of involvement with girls, I had always been loved by the parents and dumped by the daughters.

It took me longer to win Camille's parents than it had taken me to win her; but finally I broke them down and made them realize that Camille could be happy marrying beneath her. And soon I fell even farther beneath her when my car deposited a rod on the turnpike during one of my commutes to Maryland. For a couple of weeks, while I scraped up the money for the repair, I couldn't see Camille. I stayed in New York, missed her fiercely, and savored the thought of spending the rest of my life with a woman who would have been *happy* if I'd been a teacher and who might never ask me, *Did you win yet?* I knew now that during my three hundred nights of staking out that corner drugstore, I had been looking for so much more than a sensuous braid or a sumptuous thigh or a musical ear. I had been looking for Camille.

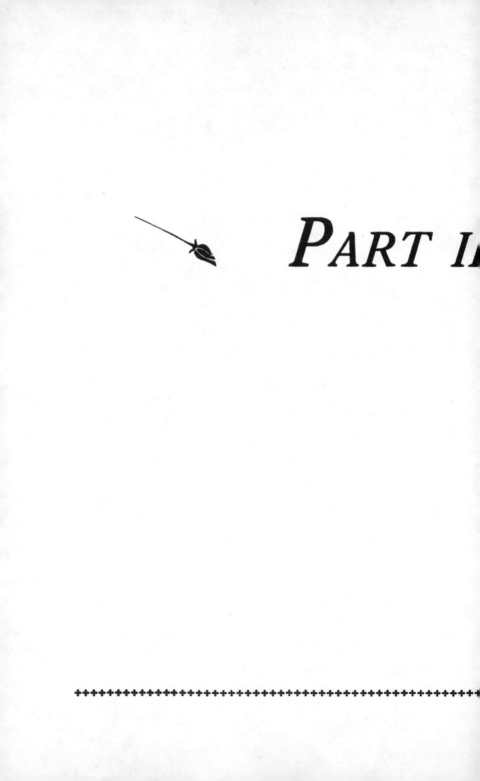

PART II

MARRIAGE

++

9

WHAT DID YOU SAY A CLOSET IS FOR?

And so, Camille and I embarked on the greatest adventure of all: a man and a woman daring to plunge into the wedded abyss and spend their entire lives together. If the amusement park called Great Adventure had been created by me, it would have no slides or rides: it would simply have one married couple trying to sustain the glow of their love while the wife gave the husband's favorite suits to the Salvation Army. For the last twenty-five years, since a certain wedding in Olney, Maryland, in 1964, the Salvation Army has been fighting Satan not only with the cross of Jesus but the cream of my coats and pants.

When I got married, one of the many things I didn't know was that Camille would grow tired of looking at some of my suits, even two I hadn't worn; but I loved her so much that I didn't mind her secretly recycling my wardrobe. I rejoiced that I now was married to the most beautiful woman I had ever seen, a woman who suddenly made Jane Russell no more alluring to me than Nipsey. My instinct was to break the rules of marriage and be honest with her about everything. I quickly realized, however, that even the deepest love doesn't stop a marriage from being a constant struggle for control. Any husband who says, "My wife and I are completely equal partners" is talking either about a law firm or a hand of bridge.

Yes, let us now set forth one of the fundamental truths about marriage: the wife is in charge. Or, to put it another way, the husband is not. Now I can hear your voices crying out:

What patronizing nonsense.
What a dumb generalization.
What a great jacket for the Salvation Army.

Well, my proof of the point is a simple one. If any man truly believes that he is the boss of his house, then let him do this: pick up the phone, call a wallpaper store, order new wallpaper for one of the rooms in his house, and then put it on. He would have a longer life expectancy sprinkling arsenic on his eggs. Any husband who buys wallpaper, drapes, or even a prayer rug on his own is auditioning for the Bureau of Missing Persons.

Therefore, in spite of what Thomas Jefferson wrote, all men may be created equal, but not to all women, and the loveliest love affair must bear the strain of this inequality once the ceremony is over. When a husband and wife settle down together, there is a natural struggle for power (I wonder why he bothers); and in this struggle, the husband cannot avoid giving up a few things—for example, dinner.

To be fair, I must admit that Camille did wait a few years before allowing me to make this particular sacrifice. I had just sat down at the table one night with her and our three children when I happened to notice that my plate contained only collard greens and brown rice.

"Would you please donate this to the Hare Krishna and bring me my real meal," I said to the gentleman serving the food.

"You have it all," he replied.

"No, what I have is a snack for the North Korean Army. The meat must have slipped off somewhere. Why don't we try to find it together?"

"Mrs. Cosby said we are no longer eating meat."

"She *did?*" I looked down the table at Camille. "Dear, if I got a letter from the Pope, do you think I could—"

"Bill, meat is bad for us and we just have to cut it

out. It's full of fat that could kill you. I'm sorry I forgot to tell you."

"So am I. I could've started eating out at a place where they don't mind who they kill."

"Honey, *lots* of people are vegetarians."

"And lots of people like to get hit with whips, but I've managed to be happy not joining them."

Nevertheless, I became a vegetarian. A husband should go with the flow of his marriage, even when that flow leads over a cliff.

About two years later, however, I sat down to dinner one night and a steak suddenly appeared on my plate.

"Look at this," I said to the gentleman serving the food. "Someone has lost a steak. Would you please return it to its owner."

"Mrs. Cosby said we are eating meat again," he told me.

"How nice to see the cows come home," I said.

The unexpected return of the cows that night taught me an important lesson about marriage: just when you think you know all there is to know about your mate, just when you think you have enough to begin the divorce, something new pops up to bewilder you, for men and women belong to different species and communication between them is a science still in its infancy.

++

For example, one of my many charming idiosyncrasies is that I rarely put my shoes in my closet. I don't put them in the freezer or the microwave: I merely leave them on the floor wherever I happen to take them off. Camille, however, like most women, cannot understand my carpet collection.

"Bill, I really wish you'd stop leaving your shoes all over the floor," she said one afternoon early in our marriage.

"You planning to clean the rugs?" I replied.

"No, it's because I *trip* over them."

"Well, let me ask you this."

"Please don't."

"Do you ever trip over the coffee table?"

"No, but—"

"And you never trip on the dog or the children. But you trip on my shoes."

"Well, first of all, I always know where the coffee table is."

"And the dog files a flight plan with you? The children show up on your radar? Dear, you don't have to be Edwin Moses to go over a pair of shoes."

"Bill, I need the *other* Moses to part all the shoes you leave lying around. When we got married, you didn't tell me that you don't believe in closets."

Camille and I had this philosophical dialogue many times, but I never changed the habit because changing a habit violates the entire tradition of marriage.

✦✦

And then one day, I took off my shoes in the living room, went to the kitchen to make some coffee, and returned to the living room to find that the shoe fairy had come but forgotten to leave a dollar.

"Dear," I said to Camille, "in your travels around, did you happen to see my shoes?"

"Constantly," she said. "They are part of the decor. This house is done in early footwear."

"Well, in case I ever want to put them on again—perhaps to go out and see a lawyer—could you tell me where they are?"

"Bill, if you really want to take off your shoes so much, why don't you go to Japan?"

"I would if I could find my shoes."

When you first begin sleeping with your wife, all your moves are like Michael Jordan's because the glow of being deeply in love gives delight to even the nonsexual gymnastics in bed. For example, in the early days of our marriage, Camille used to sleep with her back against me and I often put my leg over her. In those days, no physical position, no matter how awkward, was anything but enchanted entanglement.

"I love your knee in my groin, darling," she would say. "Care to put the other in one of my kidneys?"

"As soon as I can find it, dear," I'd reply.

"Is your arm okay like that? I mean, it'll snap back, won't it?"

"It was worse in the Bucknell game."

"What a precious man. Now you tell me the *moment* it starts to die."

How romantic are these early marital contortions that merrily sprain you. However, by your fifteenth year . . .

"Is that your *leg* on me?" your beloved inquires.

"It's not the Abominable Snowman," you sweetly reply.

"No, it's another guy with a weight problem."

"I love your easy wit."

"How easy will it be for you to remove that leg?"

"Oh, I—"

"Are you really that anxious to climb something?"

"Dear, I'm just doing what we—"

" 'Cause you can call the Explorers Club."

As the years of our marriage have passed, Camille and I have grown closer in mind and heart but not in sleep. At the beginning, I would leave our bed to go to the bathroom and she would half-awaken and say with a smile, "Have a good trip, darling. And hurry home."

If, instead of taking a trip, I had put on the light to read or shoot a few baskets, she never complained.

"What time is it?" she would say when the light hit her face.

"Three A.M.," I'd reply. "You don't have to get up yet. Isn't that good news?"

"Yes, and I love you for telling me. I wonder why I woke up."

"Just your body's natural rhythm."

By our fifteenth year, however, we were no longer in sync in the sack. And today, she will turn to me while I'm reading and say, "Now hear this. It is time to go to sleep."

"Just another hour or two," I'll reply. "I want to see if Scarlett's side wins the war."

"Bill, you know I can't sleep with the light on. If you love me, the least you could do is try to read with it off. Or maybe get under the covers with a flashlight. Pretend you're at camp."

"Yes, Stalag 17."

"Very well, I see I won't get anywhere with the old male stubbornness. I'll just go down and sleep on the couch."

"Dear," I now will say, turning out the light, "did you know that Winston Churchill said he owed the success of his marriage to never sleeping in the same room as his wife?"

"I knew he was great for something more than just defeating Hitler," she will say.

Not only is a marriage strained through the years

by one of you wanting to see in the bedroom, but there is also a change that both of you have in your view of snoring. In the early years, snoring by one of you moves the listener to gently touch the other and say, "Honey, you're snoring. Not that I *mind* it, of course—in fact, it's a Mozart serenade—but medical studies have revealed that there's a certain harm to the snorer. Something about the vibration dislodging the brain."

And the snorer smilingly replies, "Did I ever tell you how much I love you when you wake me from a deep sleep? I really hate sleeping too long at one time because it keeps me away from you."

After fifteen years, however, the snorer is not only touched: he is rolled onto the floor. Because he is familiar with the layout of the bedroom, he usually manages to find his way back into bed, where he picks up the beat with his nose. The listener then simply puts a pillow over his face, a move that stops the snoring but does cause the nuisance of having to check from time to time to see if the snoring has stopped because the snorer has died.

The timeless question that no philosopher has ever been able to answer is not: Why is Atlanta in the Western Division? And it is not: Why did the Lord have to give mankind *both* locusts and lawyers? The unanswerable question is: Does a husband have the

+++

right to see the road to the toilet at two o'clock in the morning or does his marital vow oblige him to walk into the wall?

"What's wrong—a *burglar?*" Camille suddenly says when I try to turn on my lamp so that all of the light hides on my side of the bed.

"No problem, dear. I appreciate your help, but I can do this alone."

"Do what?"

"Go to the bathroom."

"And you need a light show for it?"

"Well, I don't want to urinate in the closet."

"You already *went* to the bathroom once tonight."

"I didn't know you were scoring. You getting ready to referee a steroids test?"

When she laughs, I know that I have gotten a release from jail and I walk to the bathroom with glee, tripping only once on my shoes.

A new challenge, however, arises an hour later, when I want to slip out of bed again to get some water, watch some TV, and shoot a few baskets. In the dark stillness of the bedroom, I lie frozen and wonder: Is the radar screen still on? What would be the price of an attempted escape?

At last, I summon the courage to roll out of bed and onto the floor, like a Navy frogman hitting the water; and then I quickly crawl toward the kitchen, hoping that the thud has not awakened the Grand Inquisitor.

✦✦

If there is one thing that marriage requires, it is adjustment, especially to making a silent predawn escape from your beloved looking like a cocker spaniel.

But the adjustment is gradual and not connected to the love. In fact, through all the years of my marriage, my love for Camille, like my stomach, has steadily grown. And strangely enough, this growth has violated a mathematical principle because there was no room for it: when I married Camille, my love for her was an absolute. I was living the lyrics of the corniest songs, for I was ready to climb the highest mountain for her and to swim the deepest ocean.

After twenty-five years, however, the paradoxical truth is that I love her even more than I did when my love was absolute, but what I will climb for her now is lower than Everest; and as for a swim in her honor, I would like to make it a lap.

What she *wants* me to climb, of course, is anything but her. It is poignant to see me night after night trying to recapture the sweetness of our first easy gymnastics in bed, to see me night after night trying to slip my leg over her only to hear, "I was wondering something: Do I happen to look like a pack mule to you? Is my next birthday present going to be a saddle?"

I may have to take a trip to Tibet for an explanation of the mystical nature of our relationship, for I am more in love with Camille today than I have ever been and she is more in love with me too; but her offbeat ways of showing this love sometimes seem to contain a message to get lost.

How warmly I remember the days when Camille and I were newlyweds and she would turn on her side in bed and I would fit myself against her as neatly as a Lego. We would fall asleep that way; and whenever she rolled, I rolled too, like a new Olympic event called synchronized sack.

"Are you comfortable, sweetheart?" I would say as I put her into a loving half nelson.

"Oh, yes," she would reply. "There's no such word as 'discomfort' when I'm all wrapped up by you."

But fifteen years later, my wrap party got a different review.

"Hey, octopus," she now would say, "are you comfortable?"

"I'm in heaven," I would reply.

"Well, *I'm* in a much lower region. But that's okay. I'll just lie here and work on my soul because suffering is supposed to be good for it."

She is, however, selective about the suffering I inspire in her: some of it does not seem soul stirring enough to take.

"Where are you going?" I say to her as she gets up from a dinner table and starts to leave people I'm entertaining.

"To anyplace," she softly says, "where I won't have to hear this story for the ninety-seventh time."

This moment reveals the ultimate challenge for a woman in marriage: to accept it for the rerun it is but keep herself from canceling the show.

Camille, unfortunately, isn't equal to the challenge: she requires fresh entertainment; she wants to be seeing things for the first time; and baseball is one such thing. She has seen parts of hundreds of games, each time with the understanding of someone who just stepped off a flight from Mars.

For example, one evening, I was sitting in my living room and watching the playoffs between the Los Angeles Dodgers and the New York Mets.

"Keep that on," said Camille, entering the room.

"You don't want the Home Shopping Network?" I said.

"No, this is what I like: the World Series."

"It's the playoffs."

"Same thing."

"That's what I was about to say."

"This is when it *means* something," she said. "You know all those other games they play?"

"You mean the season?"

"Right. Well, I don't know why they play them."

"Just something to do to warm up for the playoffs, I guess."

+++

"Well, I just can't get involved in them because they don't *mean* anything."

"Yes, I frankly don't see how the players manage to pay attention either."

Moments later, Mookie Wilson hit a meaningful grounder to deep short, sprinted to first, and beat the throw. Then he stopped running, turned, and walked slowly back to the bag.

"*Tag* him! *Tag* him!" cried Camille.

"For any particular reason?" I said.

"Of course! He ran past the base and he's *out!*"

"No, dear, you're *allowed* to overrun first."

"Since when?"

"Since 1869."

"Well, not everybody knows about it."

"You really don't love this game, do you?" I said.

"Frankly, it's for little boys. But all men are little boys, so I understand. You're just trying to relive your boyhood fantasies."

"No, my boyhood fantasy wasn't to play in the major leagues. My boyhood fantasy was to marry a woman who knew you can overrun first base."

10

—

YOUR BELOVED FOE

"I was married once," says a man in *The Importance of Being Earnest*. "It was the result of a misunderstanding between myself and a young woman."

Misunderstanding does unfortunately lie at the heart of marriage, for no matter how deeply a man and woman love each other, they are often like two UN delegates whose headphones have jammed. They are constantly finding common ground that turns out to be quicksand.

A few years ago, Camille would happily have gone into quicksand rather than into the sauna I had built for our house in Los Angeles.

"That steam room," she said right after it had been completed. "Are you planning to do your own dry cleaning?"

+++

"It'll be dry cleaning *us*," I replied. "It's for *you* and *me*."

"Honey, *I* can't take that much heat."

"It'll be a complete rebirth for you."

"Have I complained about the first one? Bill, those saunas go up to a hundred and twenty *degrees*."

"But it's so healthful," I said, aware of my marital duty to keep educating my wife, but deciding not to educate her with the news that the temperature would not be a hundred and twenty: it would be a hundred and ninety-five.

"It's healthful to pass out?" she said.

"That's the wrong attitude. A sauna purges the body of all impurities. And it's not just your average hundred and twenty degrees; it's *dry* heat."

"Let's put it this way: it's not the heat, it's the stupidity."

"Millions of *Finns* do it. They not only do it, but they roll in the snow afterward."

"And that's why Finland never wins a war."

In spite of Camille's objection, my blend of intellect and charm was persuasive enough to lure her into trying the new sauna with me. This woman did, after all, have courage: she had passed up countless breadwinners to marry a nightclub comedian.

And so, together we took off our clothes and walked into a six-by-six wooden room that conjured up visions of a Russian prison sentence.

+++

"Now just remember, dear," I said as the waves of heat began striking us, "that this is good for the *skin.* It gets out the dirt."

"That's what they told Joan of Arc," she said.

It was deeply moving to see what my wife was doing in the name of love. After ten minutes, the temperature was a hundred and forty five, but luckily Camille couldn't see the thermometer because her eyes were rolling back in her head.

"Bill, I think that's enough for today," she said, falling against the door and opening it. "My dermatologist likes me medium-rare."

"But you're missing the full benefit," I told her.

"Why don't we try to get that in a picnic at Death Valley next week?"

Teaching your wife little things, like how to broil herself or brush her teeth, is a form of education that can move the student to throw something at you. And once something is thrown at you, there is liable to be a fight. The experts on marriage, most of whom are divorced, like to say that marital fighting is good because it clears the air; but it seems to me that such fighting often leaves the air quality as unacceptable as it was when your wife happened to say:

"I think you should know I'm really tired of your always saying that I'm an urban village idiot."

"No, dear," you reply, "you're not paying attention.

I don't *always* say that you're an urban village idiot. I have said it only *twice:* last Tuesday evening at your mother's and last May seventeenth at church. Our relationship would be stronger if you kept better score."

"And you *always* correct me like that."

"No, again not *always:* just the few thousand times when you're wrong."

"But I'm *not* wrong. I remember *precisely* what you've said to me."

"No, you remember *imprecisely* what I've said to you. Or else precisely what some *other* husband has said."

"You never *listen* to me."

"You're nothing-for-three today. The truth is, I probably listen too much. I should be more selective."

"You know what I've decided?"

"What?"

"That you're the most irritating man in the world."

"You've got to watch those generalizations. The most irritating man in the world is Mr. Botha."

"Who's Prince Charming compared to *you.* Oh, how I wish I had tapes of our conversations to prove to you what you really said."

"*Your* half belongs on 'The Twilight Zone.' Which is where I think I'm living sometimes. Just tell me this:

Did you happen to move my collection of hand grenades from my table in the den?"

"Yes, I did."

"And do you happen to remember where you put
them?"

"The same way I remember everything you say. I
put them in the attic."

"You doing some decorating up there?"

"Down *here* they were in the way."

"In the way of *what?* A plate of Swedish meatballs?
A picture of Wilt Chamberlain? Those hand grenades
were souvenirs and they were *mine.* You just can't
keep on hiding my things. I walk around this house
looking for my things like somebody who's lost his
mind."

"Yes, that *is* your best imitation."

This kind of heartfelt give-and-take is what the matrimonial sages say will bring you two closer together.
And often it does: often the combat leads to a peace
conference that is sexually delicious. In building to
this conference, however, you have to fight fairly,
keep your obscenities polite, and remember how precious you are to each other, even though you both are
thinking:

That's it! *There is no way I can continue living with
this person. I want to live with something better, like a
gerbil.*

If the fighting is to lead to the climax of a passion-

+++

ate embrace, then the man must be careful never to say the five words that launched the Women's Movement:

"Are you expecting your period?"

These are the last five words that Samson said to Delilah. They are the words that were spoken one day to a young Fall River lady named Lizzie Borden. They are the words that have moved luggage from closets to front doors all over the world.

This question *is* a very tempting weapon for the American fighting man because women are prone to irrationality just before menstruation. Men, on the other hand, have a nice evenness to their irrationality. They can be just as crazy at Easter as they are on Veterans Day.

It is, of course, not always possible for your wife to leave you during a fight because sometimes the fight has been in a car and she would find no comfort fleeing to the shoulder of I-95. For some reason, a car is the scene of matrimonial highs and lows. Early in your marriage, the two of you exchange endearing smiles when you are driving along and your wife suddenly says, "Look out for that armored column!"

"What a thoughtful and sharp-eyed sweetheart you are to take the trouble to point out all those slowly approaching tanks," you reply. "I probably would've seen them on my own and they're probably friendly and they're probably stopping at the light, but your spotting them for me still makes my heart hum like the engine of a Rolls."

Later in the marriage, however, the same helpful tip brings a different response from you at the wheel.

"Look out for that armored column!" she says.

"You think I don't *see* it?" you reply.

"I'm never sure *what* you see."

"I'm starting to see bachelorhood in a whole new light."

Moreover, your automotive rapport suffers the same decline during the years that the two of you keep trying to navigate toward unknown destinations. Early in the marriage, it is gaily romantic for the two of you to get lost together, just as it was a merry moment when Columbus told his first mate, "India, Youngstown, who *cares* as long as we're having fun!"

"Darling," your young wife says, "please understand the spirit in which I say this: I think Chicago was a *left* at that fork."

"I took a shot," you reply, "just as I did when I married you. Maybe I'll luck out again."

And she laughs and puts her befuddled head against your uncertain steering arm and says, "Getting there with you is half the fun, even if we're going nowhere."

✦✦

However, later in the marriage, getting lost is less enchanting.

"You missed the turn, Magellan," she says. "Chicago was a *left* at that fork. Or are you trying to get there by way of Montreal?"

"No, it was a *right* at the fork," you reply, "but thanks anyway for the misinformation. Why don't you just concentrate on holding the change for the tolls?"

"Why don't *you* concentrate on changing from someone who always yells at me?"

"I don't *always* yell at you. You call just twenty-three times this week *always?*"

An interesting thing has happened. Two different arguments have converged: the one about your always doing something and the one about your recently taking the wrong turn. And at the convergence are the tears of your wife.

"Now, crying doesn't make you right," you say. "It just stuffs you up so you hear even less of the wisdom I keep trying to impart to you. If you'd just start *listening* to me, you'd learn—"

"I don't want to learn from you 'cause I don't want a diploma in wrong turns! You make me feel like I'm stupid when *you're* the one who doesn't know how to drive!"

"Let me ask you a question that even *you* might be able to answer: Did you ever wonder why they put all

+++

the instruments on *this* side of the car? They put them here for *me* because this is where I'm sitting. There's no copilot in these things."

"And did *you* ever wonder why you didn't pull over to the first gas station and get proper directions for Chicago instead of wandering around like Moses in the wilderness?"

"Because I know what I'm doing."

"What you're doing is getting lost and I'm not talking to you anymore."

"Is that a promise?"

"So many men I could have married and I had to pick the happy wanderer."

"All right, let's try it *your* way," you say, swerving into a service station. "Let's ask *him.*"

"No, not *him,*" she says.

"Why?"

"Because he doesn't look as though he knows."

"But he looks as though he did well on the SATs."

"I tell you he's weak on geography."

And off you go, moving farther away from both your destination and each other.

Suddenly, you come to a sign: NOT A THROUGH STREET.

"This street looks good," you say. "That sign is just to keep out the trucks."

"If this doesn't work," she says, "you can turn into the next black hole."

✦✦

A half hour later, when you reach a gas attendant whose face reveals a high IQ to your wife, you receive the right instructions, but they lack a certain value because you have listened to only every fifth word: "Hang a left . . . hang a right . . . hang yourself . . ."

"Well, what do we do *now*, Mrs. Navigator?" you ask your wife when you arrive at the Mexican border.

"How do *I* know? *You're* Mr. Iacocca. I told you: I'm not even in the car with you anymore."

"Don't tease me with my dreams."

When you finally arrive at your destination two days later, you are silent enemies. The fight will resume, of course, after your visit, unless you wisely abandon the car and come home by bus. Even in a bus, however, the battle might still flare up again and the other passengers might have to listen to endless themes and variations of the two lines that are the favorites in most marital fights:

THE HUSBAND: That's not what I'm *saying.*

THE WIFE: Then what's your *point?*

THE HUSBAND: My point is that's not what I'm *saying.*

THE WIFE: Do you think that you'll ever be saying your *point?* Or would you rather get a pencil and paper and try *drawing* it?

Camille and I once accidentally switched these two lines because we'd forgotten our parts during a long spell of peace, but I found that I didn't have my heart in asking her what was her point, and she seemed to lack a flair for telling me what she was saying. She seemed uncomfortable trying to clarify a thought that she probably wanted to keep obscure.

Reading the wrong dialogue is bad enough, but going blank is even worse. The argument I dislike most is the one in which Camille just suddenly walks away from me and I forget my next line. When she returns, I can either vamp until I remember what I was talking about or I can start a new fight about her halftime break.

"That was really lovely to just walk out that way," I once told her.

"I thought I'd do some shopping while you were trying to find your point," she said.

In my twenty-five years on the roller coaster of marriage, I have discovered that marital fights sometimes last for three or four days because the opponents aren't playing the same game: men and women fight differently. For example, at certain times in a fight a woman likes to respond by sticking her fingers in her ears, but a man does this only to catch mosquitoes.

"Now *that's* truly adult," you say. "Just tuning out . . . Did you *hear* me? I said, 'That's truly adult.' "

And then she starts to hum, but not even one of your favorite tunes, just something that *sounds* like a mosquito. She not only is hearing nothing from you, but she is also broadcasting a noise that brings to your mind the part of the marriage vow covering "for better or worse." It rarely gets much worse than this —except perhaps the night that I was reading in the den and she came in, went to the thermostat, turned up the heat, and started to leave.

"Hey there," I said. "I'm here. Perhaps you didn't see me sitting here and quietly improving my mind."

"I saw you," she replied.

"Well, perhaps you didn't know that the temperature was quite comfortable for me. In fact, I was just telling myself: 'Bill, you don't have to take a vacation because you're already in a place where the heat is just right.'"

"You don't know if a room is hot or cold."

Now this indeed was a memorable moment. My wife is surely more intelligent than I am because she knows what to tell the children to keep them from putting holes in each other, but even *my* modest IQ usually lets me know if a room is hot or cold. And so, what does a man do when his wife feels he needs a class in remedial thermostat reading?

If I were smarter, I would know.

Ever since Socrates' wife told him to go and seek the truth in another house, philosophers have debated whether a husband and wife should go to bed angry at each other. There are two sound reasons for making up at bedtime: it feels like the right moment for reconciliation and a fight is harder to sustain when one of the fighters falls asleep. In fact, there is nothing more maddening than finally finding the words you've been looking for—*That's not what I'm saying*—and then having to deliver them to an unconscious foe, who cannot ask you, *Then what's your point?* Do you wake her up to hear your words, thus taking a chance on learning what it feels like to be part of a justifiable homicide? Or do you save the words until morning, when she will have even less idea of what you're talking about?

In spite of the beauty of our love, Camille and I have had bedtimes never discussed by Mister Rogers. Like two heavyweights going for the title, we enter the downy ring and then turn away from each other and move to our corners. And now I start thinking of all the people I could have married who kept their fingers out of their ears and who would have let me try to figure out all by myself if I was cold. Denise, Artemis, Rosemary, Charlene, Lori, Millie, Sarah, Ruth . . . They may have been dumb about sports or had no taste in music or liked stolen jewelry, but all of them are suddenly looking like Whitney Houston to me.

+++

I'm not going to touch her, I think, as the two of us lie there in stony silence. *I won't even shake hands with her lawyer. And if she touches* me, *I'll wash it off with Brillo.*

But then her heel grazes mine and this least erogenous part of her calls up a memory so sweet that it almost stops me from trying to fill her with guilt.

"If you don't want me in this bed," I quietly tell her, "just say the word."

"Don't let *me* keep you from leaving," she replies.

"Just say the word."

"If you have travel plans . . ."

"Just say the word."

"Have a good trip."

"All right, I know a hint when I hear one. I'll just sleep on the floor. I'll pretend I'm back in the Army."

"You were in the Navy."

"Whatever. Okay, I'll be hitting the deck now. That's the sound you'll be hearing."

When I finally do drop to the floor, there is a certain loss of dignity. On the other hand, I have strengthened my bargaining position for pity.

"Camille?"

"Yes, sailor?"

"You just going to leave me down here?"

"I don't vacuum till Tuesday."

"Just leave me down here like an old bear rug?"

"Bear? You know what I can't *bear?* The way you're always such a . . . such a . . . *man.* Only a *man* would think that moving to a lower level makes him right."

"Well, I just want to say one more thing that happens to *be* right: I love you."

"See? If you talk long enough, you finally make sense. And I love you."

"Well, sending me to the floor isn't the tenderest way to show it."

"Honey, you booked that trip yourself."

"Sometimes you take me for granted, you know. There are plenty of other women who'd have me and never move me to the floor."

"*Plenty* of other women? Name *one* of 'em who'd take a man who spends half the day looking for his glasses and the other half looking for his keys." She began to laugh. "And this man can find his keys only if he finds his glasses first."

"At least I have missions in life," I say, climbing back into bed and moving toward her. "A man has to—"

"Just close your mouth and kiss me and stop trying to explain men. Let a veterinarian do that."

"I'll bet Charlene is still waiting for me," I say, drawing her into an embrace that has made the whole battle worthwhile.

+++

"Charlene . . ." says Camille after releasing my lips. "Was she the one who pretended that she liked John Coltrane? Or was she the one whose head you almost took off at the track meet?"

11

To LOVE. HONOR. AND DRIVE UP THE WALL

Camille is so concerned about my well-being that she sometimes goes even beyond teaching me how to tell hot from cold. She also teaches me how to know when nighttime comes—knowledge that is valuable not only to fireflies.

She begins the lesson by walking into the room where I am sitting and closing the blinds.

"Please do something else," I tell her, "like punish the children or lube the car."

"It's time to close the blinds," she says.

"Is that something official, like Daylight Savings Time?"

"No, it's just time to close the blinds."

"It is six-fifteen in this room and three-fifteen in San Francisco, but neither time means a thing be-

++

cause I don't *want* the blinds closed. I want to look out. And *you* better look out too."

I am, however, filled with nostalgia for the blind closing at those other times when Camille enters a room where I'm sitting, turns out the lights, and starts to leave.

"Hey, I'm *here,*" I say, "and I'm *reading*—when I can see the page, that is."

"You may be here," she replies, "but you're not all there. You were sleeping."

"If I was sleeping, how did I know you were here?"

"You don't know if you're reading or sleeping."

At once, I take out my wallet and check my age to see if I've already gone past kindergarten. For some reason that neither Margaret Mead nor Oprah Winfrey has ever discovered, a wife often treats her husband as if he were one of her pupils in a kindergarten class. She doesn't make him lie down on a blanket at noon or pin a paper flower to his shirt with his name, but she does often presume that he hasn't yet mastered the art of thinking for himself.

For example, at a dinner party one night, I saw a hostess offer a second portion of potatoes to a man whose wife then said, "Oh, Sam won't have any more."

A woman like that deserves a note in her bed saying: SAM WON'T HAVE ANY MORE. On the other hand, Sam was probably doing some things to drive his teacher crazy, like constantly scratching the back of his head or constantly jiggling his leg, two accomplished tics of mine that have made Camille wonder if marriage might be an unnatural state for human beings.

For our first few years together, Camille said nothing about my scratching the back of my head or my jiggling leg, perhaps because she was impressed that a man of my modest intellect was able to do them both at once. However, one day shortly after we had celebrated our tenth anniversary, I was busy scratching the back of my head when she suddenly said, "Please stop *doing* that."

"Doing what?" I replied with a scratch of my head.

"Scratching the back of your head; it drives me crazy."

"I'm sorry, dear. I didn't know you were emotionally involved with my scratching."

"Is it rotten shampoo or are you trying to show that you're thinking?"

In the following days, I did no head scratching, but I missed this little workout, so I intensified my other major indoor exercise: jiggling my leg while I sat. In fact, I now was jiggling my leg hard enough to make an approach to the Richter scale.

One afternoon I was sitting and jiggling, trying to move a coffee table farther from the door, when Camille came flying at me like a safety in a goal-line stand. With both hands, she slammed down my leg and I wondered if there would be a flag on the play.

"Stop that!" she cried. "It drives me crazy!"

"I have an idea," I said, massaging my leg. "Why don't we both make lists of the things the other one does that drive us crazy."

"Make *lists?*" she asked.

"Yes, and then we could see which ones we could—"

"That drives me crazy, you know."

"What?"

"Making lists of things that drive us crazy. It takes all the romance out of marriage when you give it a scorecard."

"Anyway, you know what's funny?" I said. "I can't think of a single thing for my list."

"Oh, that's *sweet.*"

"May I jiggle now?"

Camille and I do have many things in common besides our both being afraid of the children; but our maddening traits are also there and have made me wonder from time to time if I should keep coming to a bed that can become a launching pad. For two people in a marriage to live together day after day is unquestionably the one miracle that the Vatican has overlooked. Turning water into wine was routine compared to my staying with a woman who noisily sucks air through her teeth whenever she thinks that I'm in the mood to go insane. This sound, which can drive me up the wall past the pictures, was not invented by Camille; it is a major female weapon that should have been banned by the Geneva Convention.

I hear the sound with a brain already in conflict with itself: one side, full of hope, saying, *I love her so much I don't care if she is always on Fiji time or if she thinks football is played in the spring;* but the other side of my brain, full of reality, is saying, *First my* mother *molded me for twenty-five years and now* she's *molding me for another fifty, but the role in life I had planned for myself was not a piece of Silly Putty.* Of course, the reality side also recognizes all the times that we rub each other the *right* way, all those lovely back rubs in bed at night.

In discussing his marriage, a journalist named Michael Grant has said, "We continue to adjust to each other, but don't mistake it for a solid marriage. There is no such thing. Marriage is more like an airplane than a rock."

Well, *his* marriage may be like an airplane, but mine is the *Hindenburg:* floating grandly through the fog, full of hot air and music, ready to explode. I am certain that I have one of America's better marriages; and yet the challenge of keeping it successful never dims, for Camille and I may be blinded by love, but we have Braille for each other's flaws. When I told

her that I couldn't think of a single thing for my idiosyncrasy list, I was telling a gallant lie. On such a list,
perhaps number two with a bullet just behind her
sucking air, would be her asking me every night for
twenty-five years, right after I have kissed her and
said how much I've missed her all day, "Did you lock
up?"

I do not require her to reply to my affection in By-
ronic couplets, but "Did you lock up?" closes the flue
on the fire of romance. Were I then to try to rekindle
the fire by saying, *Dear, I've locked* you *in my heart,*
she might decide to have *me* locked up; and so, I simply say, "Yes, I did."

"Did you really?"

She now has implied that my answer was a guess.

"Yes, really."

At this point in our little performance in the theater
of the absurd, she will not say, *I don't believe you;* but
a few minutes later, she will go downstairs and check
all the locks. It is nothing personal: it is simply that
women do not trust people of a foreign sex.

At bedtime I have never asked Camille, *Did you
lock up?* because I don't want to hear her say, *Of*
course *not. That's* your *job.*

The second entry on my top twenty idiosyncrasy
list would be one I have already mentioned; and my
repeating it would move Camille to say, *You* always
mention entry two.

+++

It may well be a habit of females to base sweeping accusations on one or two instances. (I can hear Gloria Steinem crying, *You men* always *say we generalize about you.*) Or such generalizing may merely be a dramatic device developed by Camille. I know only that eighteen years ago, I lost a key; and ever since then, she has handed down to the children, like an Arthurian legend: *Your father* always *loses his keys.*

Because of this legend, I've been forbidden to have a key to my house, for I am a man who cannot keep one, a man who probably would give it to the first needy person I saw on the street. Therefore, if no one is home, the silence in the house will not be broken by me because I cannot get in. If an emergency happens to arise, there is a person nearby with the keys to my house who will *let me in* but who will not *give me the keys.* In fact, on one occasion, I found myself locked *in* the house because the nearby person had let me in and then left with the keys, a moment that made me think about the deeper meaning of marriage. I realized how important it is for each partner in a marriage to make adjustments. One of mine is agreeing to live in a minimum security prison.

Camille will never apologize for treating me this way. Again, it is nothing personal; it is simply the code of wives. They do not apologize, probably because they've been spoiled by homage paid by their athletic sons. Whenever a television camera picks up a player on the sidelines after he has done something splendid, what does he say? Not *Thanks, steroids* or *That should cover the point spread* or *I'm certainly earning my salary from the school.* No, he says, *Hi, Mom,* even though Mom wishes football had never been invented by Genghis Khan.

If I ever did find myself in a real minimum security prison, visiting day would be shorter for me than for the other inmates because Camille would be half an hour late, her regular arrival time. When she finally came, of course, she would be a face worth waiting for; and when she left, right after I'd kissed her and told her how much I'd missed her, she would say, "Did you lock up?"

Camille keeps marching to a different drummer, one who missed the bus carrying the band. For example, each January she walks into the living room, sees a playoff game on the TV screen, and says, "Oh, is *this* starting again?" Like so many American wives, even those who hear *Hi, Mom,* she thinks that the football season starts with the winter playoffs and then builds to salary negotiations in the spring.

A lack of synchronization, however, between a husband and wife is something that ironically can help a marriage. If they happen to be living in two different time zones or two different seasons, their feeling for each other can be strengthened by their efforts to penetrate the other zone. Whenever I know that Camille is supposed to reach a certain place at a certain time, I call that place forty minutes late to see if she has made it. If she still isn't there, I wait another three hours, and then I begin to worry and to fantasize with a desperate heart:

> *Has she been kidnapped by gypsies or run away with the circus or simply gone someplace where nobody scratches the back of his head? Will she come home in time to buy my birthday present? Why did I ever get angry at her for a silly little thing like keeping me awake till three with her light while she read magazines and scattered cracker crumbs in the bed? I'll never get angry at her again, no matter how many really stupid things she does. I don't care if she wants to use the bed to feed pigeons, and I don't care if she says I was probably asleep all the time because I never know when I am, and I don't care if she wants me to audit a kindergarten class to learn how to lock doors. She's the best thing that ever happened to me and I want her back, even if she comes home half an hour late.*

++

With all the irregular rhythms that pulse between a husband and wife, the wonder is that any couple can sustain the glow of romance. "How do you keep the music playing?" asks the song, for so many marriages seem to be a natural segue from a waltz to "Taps."

The launching of a marriage is almost always romantic, as in the way that Ahmad Rashad, while broadcasting football, turned from Marcus Allen to Phylicia with his own game plan. The average man, of course, must do something simpler, like take an ad in the personals column saying: LUCRETIA, WILL YOU MARRY ME? OFFER GOOD UNTIL MIDNIGHT FRIDAY. PHOTO ON REQUEST. HENRY. But if things are so good between Henry and Lucretia, why is she reading the personals? And why is a man trying to understand the way of a woman? I should keep remembering what a writer named Jennifer Harlow Smith has said about the man she loves: "Romance, I realized, lay in acknowledging the mysterious *distance* between us. The sexes come from different citadels. He *thinks* differently than I. How wonderful."

Yes, wonderful at the beginning, when your life together is a romantic high, when the lyrics of the love songs are true for you and you hear yourself singing,

I didn't know what time it was,
Then I met you.

✦✦

A soulful thought. Camille, however, didn't know what time it was when she was twelve, for she is a woman who always seems to be wearing not a watch but a sundial, and the correct time made no particular impression on her when she fell in love with me.

Nonetheless, she did feel the romantic high that intoxicates most married couples and lasts between a week and five years. Sometime after the fifth year, however, or maybe the tenth . . .

I was sitting in my living room one evening in my thirteenth year of marriage, listening to a baritone sing,

> *A doll I can carry*
> *The girl that I marry*
> *Must be.*

"A *doll* he can *carry?*" said Camille from nearby. "That man wants a ten-inch woman!"

"No, dear," I said, "this is poetry and you just can't look at it that way. This is his dream. This is romance."

"This is a man who wants to carry a doll. Which is *okay*—he can carry a *koala*, but don't sing about it."

"You didn't always feel that way. Remember 'Crying in the Chapel'?"

She laughed. "Do I ever. God should've turned us into pillars of salt for what we did during that song."

++

"Too bad we weren't doing it to each other."

"Yes, as I recall, you had Miss Full-Court Press."

"She made me happy while I was crying in the chapel. She was a saint with great hips."

"Those songs seem pretty silly now."

"Not to me," I said dreamily.

"Because men are teenagers forever. Only the pimples disappear."

And then I gave her a long sweet kiss, a half-court press, while I thought, *My skin may have cleared up, but I'm glad I still have the mist in my mind.*

12

Till talk do you part

In her endless effort to bring her husband out of the cave, the American wife will tell him, "The problem with you is you are not in touch with your feelings." She will tell him this right after he has tried to shotput his son to dramatize some parental point for which mere language lacked clarity. She will tell him this right after he has kicked in the television set as a fitting response to an overtime field goal against his home team. A man can spend an entire morning creatively running amuck; and when he is finished and the foam on his lips has dried, his wife will say, "The problem with you is you are not in touch with your feelings."

Although I'm not a psychologist (my doctorate is in education, my BA in the quarter-mile), it has always

✦✦✦

seemed to me that I am nicely in touch with my feelings, one of which is an urge to bounce pass the next
woman who tells me I am not in touch with my feelings. Of course, what women often mean by this
charge is that men don't know how to cry; but crying
isn't always an indication of genuine feeling. If it
were, then Jimmy Swaggart and Tammy Faye Bakker
would be sensitivity's king and queen.

I sometimes think that women may be too involved
in revelation, that perhaps a marriage is strained by
just four words: not *The children aren't yours* but
How was your day? It is often too much pressure on a
man to ask him to keep giving the six o'clock news,
especially when the only thing to report is the
weather. What, for example, is a dentist to say when
his wife inquires, *How was your day?*

*I did six fillings, four root canals, and a small child
spat in my eye.*

Maybe the best answer a husband can give to *How
was your day?* is *I spent it dreading that question.* Or
maybe the husband should draw first and ask his
wife, How was your day? Then, however, he is liable
to hear the four grimmest words of all:

I had the children.

Camille never has to be a district attorney with me,
for she has a way to learn what I'm thinking that even
allows me to have a good meal.

"If I ever want to find out anything about you," she has said, "I'll invite five of your friends to dinner and just listen in."

By communicating indirectly, sometimes through a basketball team, Camille and I have been able to keep the mystery in our marriage, a quality that the marriage manuals consider important. Of course, these manuals say that communication is important too; and so, the answer seems to be that a couple should communicate mysteriously, each one making sure that the other rarely knows what he is talking about. Every time that Camille and I exchange *That's not what I'm* saying/*Then what's your* point?, we are moving further into foggy paradise.

In this happy pursuit of marital mystery, Camille and I sometimes *almost* have a conversation, but then she thinks better of the idea.

"I want to talk to you," she told me one evening in the kitchen.

"Fine," I said. "Let's do it right after I finish these chili dogs. I don't want to distract my mouth right now."

A few minutes later and a few pounds heavier, I walked into the living room, where she was standing by the fireplace, a stunning portrait of a great lady about to hold forth. I hoped I was equal to the subject. I hoped it was the Cleveland Browns.

++

"Here I am for the talking," I said. "What was it you wanted?"

"*You* know what I wanted," she replied. "Let's just leave it at that."

And she turned and went up to the bedroom, no doubt for a meeting with Godot.

Because Camille and I have wisely left each other in the dark so often, our marriage has been rich in surprise. It is an atmosphere in which my son can come to me and say, "Dad, I've decided I want to be more involved in politics."

"That's good," I reply.

"So I'm dropping out of college, changing my name to Raul, and joining the Contras."

"Then I guess you'll be wanting some advance allowance."

"Yes, please. Either pesos or traveler's checks."

"You know, this is . . . well, I guess you'd have to call it a surprise. *I* didn't know you wanted to become a Nicaraguan guerrilla. At least not this *semester.*"

"Well, *Mom* has known it for months."

"She has?"

"Yes, she even says the Contras are the ideal group for me because I'm always against everything. Dad, if you and Mom did more talking, you'd be ready with a going-away present for me."

My son did not understand, however, that there is a method in the intermittent and semicoherent exchanges of information that Camille and I have: we are trying not to use up the conversation allotted to our marriage. Unaware that this conversational allotment governs every marriage, most young couples do not pace their tongues and suddenly find themselves in three-month lulls.

The next time you're in a restaurant, study some couple that seems to have been married for more than ten years. Watch them exchanging long desperate looks, each of them hoping that the numbing silence will be broken by a good grease fire or a holdup. And each of them is about to be driven to think the unthinkable:

We should have brought the children.

Camille and I bring the children. In fact, people have said that we are prisoners of the children because we bring them everywhere we go, from Las Vegas to the South of France. However, I can recall six times in our marriage when we left the children home. *Seven* times if you count the night that Camille walked out on me and I went after her without bothering to get a sitter.

Nevertheless, I have to admit that whenever Camille has suggested that we go off without the children for longer than an hour and a half, I say either, "But it's always more *fun* with the children along" or "Just be patient, dear. In just nine or ten or fifteen years, they'll all be married or in the armed forces and then we'll have the house back. That's our reason to keep *living.*"

However, early one summer in our thirteenth year of marriage, my mother offered to stay with the children for a week so that Camille and I could go on a little vacation alone and recapture the magic of the honeymoon we had always planned to take. For a moment, I had considered having my mother take Camille for a week and letting *me* go off with the children, whose interests were closer to mine; but then I yielded to my yen for adventure and decided to see if Camille and I could make it alone, operating under the handicap of having to talk only to each other.

"Darling," I had said to her, "what would you say if I told you that we're going to take a vacation without the children?"

"I'd say you're a liar," she replied.

"And usually you'd be right, but my mother just offered to stay with them so we can get to know each other again—unless there's someone else you'd rather get to know."

"No, you'll do. But I thought you said it's always more fun with the kids along."

"So it won't be our greatest vacation, but at least it'll be all ours. Just the two of us, dancing away from Fat Albert."

++

As the moment of our departure approached, Camille and I conceived some rules for this romantic escapade:

♥ There could be no mention of the children.
♥ No photographs, tapes of cuteness, or report cards could be taken along.
♥ No one could become pregnant or in any other way involved with kids.

And so, one afternoon in July, we turned our two girls and our boy over to my mother and then drove out to a charming old inn on eastern Long Island. A few minutes after arriving, as I zipped up the back of Camille's dress before taking her to an elegant dinner, I said, "You look so young and lovely. No one could ever tell that you have two kid . . . um, kidneys. Sorry."

"That's okay," she said. "I miss them too, those precious kidneys. And that spleen."

"Courage," I said. "We can make it."

In the dining room, we found a corner table, where I sat down and began desperately trying to think of things to talk about. So far, I had two: the plight of the dollar and the plight of the whale. I would have to pace myself with them or my mouth would be retired before the soup.

After a silence of no more than five or ten minutes,

I tenderly placed my hand on Camille's and said, "Have I ever told you, my darling, that they should let the dollar float?"

"How you *talk,* lover," she demurely replied.

"And speaking of floating, this is a tough time to be a whale, don't you think?"

She smiled helplessly, and then I said, "You look so young and lovely tonight."

"You've said that already, but I don't mind. If my loveliness is the bottom of your barrel, you can go with it for a day or two."

The pressure was getting to me now. How *could* parents keep themselves from talking about their children? I decided that there should be a clinic where addicts could taper off, first looking at photos of their own children, then gradually at someone else's, and finally at slides of vasectomies.

Once our appetizers came, we began to chew our way through a seemingly endless lull. I thought about my oldest daughter often telling me not to talk with a mouthful of food and I congratulated myself on avoiding a demerit from Camille by keeping the thought unexpressed.

"You know, the Owls could go all the way this year," I finally said.

"Some new migration?" she replied.

"The *Temple* Owls. All the way."

"That would be nice. All the way where?"

++

As a bird-watcher, Camille was no better than Denise. Was *any* woman wise enough to follow my Owls?

After the meal a romantic mood was upon us, so hand in hand we walked down to the beach under a sky full of stars. We went almost to the water's edge, and for four or five minutes nothing was said; but neither of us was trying now, for we both were transported by the awesome beauty of the universe. At last, however, from somewhere deep in my soul, a thought emerged and was given voice.

"Just think," I said. "At this very moment, under these very stars, a little Cosby is wetting the bed." And then I piteously cried, "Oh, honey, I *tried!* You don't *know* how I tried!"

"Don't hate yourself," she said. "I was just about to suggest that we gather some shells for them."

13

La DIFFÉRENCE

In Chapter Seven, I said that men and women are very different, a philosophical insight you also can find in *The Collected Wisdom of Bugs Bunny*, but one that is still worth saying again. Now before Camille tells me *You* always *make this point in* all *the chapters of* all *your books*, let me remind her that it never appeared in *Picture Pages*; and then let me explain my single repetition of it here: because this fundamental truth—that women are not just men who can have babies and men are not just women who spike footballs—gives marriage its vitality, its dynamics, its delights, and its divorce. Americans may like the style called unisex, but the wiser French have a devout appreciation of the wonder they call *la différence.*

✦✦

A few years ago, a book called *Sex and the Brain* said that not only are the sexes profoundly different, but these differences are in the brain before birth and are not taught by society. There is no society where women learn to have a keener sense of smell than men, to play worse chess than men, to stand more pain than men, to write less music than men, and to do better than men in elementary school.

When my youngest daughter was in the first grade at an all-girls' school, I went to her class one day and watched twenty-five girls of six and seven sitting in silent attention for fifteen minutes.

"To get twenty-five boys to do that," the teacher told me, "you'd have to put Thorazine in their milk."

Do boys *study* short attention spans? Do their fathers *teach* them to squirm and to run into walls?

Yes, the differences between the partners in a marriage start early, run deep, and have little to do with environment because the environment that counts most is the womb. As another example, girls almost always walk and talk sooner than boys. However, since society has been dominated by male chauvinists for five thousand years, shouldn't these males have seen to it that their *sons* did the first walking and talking while the girls crawled around in silence for as long as possible?

And could any man ever learn that mystical thing called woman's intuition, which isn't mystical at all but rather an ability to pick up and process subtle clues that men lack because we're kind of dense? Scientists now feel that the reason for such radar is anatomical: a larger bridge between the two sides of the female brain. To a husband in a fight with his wife, this is a bridge over troubled water; but the fight may have started because he was being blunt while she was using the subtle indirections of the female mind. Of course, it also may have started because she directly told him that he was what was wrong with America, and parts of Mexico too. And it may end when she cries, for which no penalty flag will be thrown because chemical warfare isn't forbidden in love.

"Women just don't play chess as well as men," a female chess champion once told me. "It has something to do with the abstract reasoning that also makes men better mathematicians."

This masculine flair for science may be what moved a young man in my daughter's second-grade class to tell her one day, "Please don't touch me. You have girl germs."

That evening, my puzzled daughter asked me, "Daddy, are there really girl germs?"

"Of course not," I replied. "There are only girl Germans. Boys just like to tease you."

"Why?"

+++

"Because girls are different and that's been confusing men for about ten thousand years."

You can see the flowering of this difference when you have a daughter who enters her teens, a period dangerous to mental health—both hers and yours. I have four daughters, the most precious portfolio a man can hold, and I have watched with amusement and dismay as each of them entered a period when a hair drier and a telephone became a basic life-support system.

Needless to say, the happiness of these four daughters has been of supreme importance to me, but the problem is that this happiness may depend on their avoiding the kind of person their father was in his drugstore days, a mad hunter of j-o-n-e-s. Every time a young man has come to my house for one of my daughters, I have wanted to take him aside and say:

You're not like me, are you? If you are, then I know what you want and I hope you have the same terrible luck. I hope you find my daughter a cross between Artemis and Eleanor Roosevelt. I hope you're on a mission impossible. And one more thing: I may have to kill you, but it will be nothing personal. If I don't kill you, what are your plans for the evening? Since my daughter is still a teenager and therefore won't have her mind back for another few years, I'd like you to assure me that you'll be returning here tonight in-

stead of to a disco in Guatemala. By the way, you're wearing the wrong pants.

The worst time for a father comes when his daughter is fifteen. I have now had three daughters pass through the treacherous waters of fifteen and I'm not sure I'll be strong enough to man the lighthouse for the fourth. I have heard the long phone conversations full of mournful sounds, conversations that have left my daughters looking a little less balanced than Scarlett O'Hara. I have seen them trying to learn about love, the only subject that no one has ever been able to study for.

"You know, honey," I said to one of my fifteen-year-old girls one evening, "the wisest thought about love comes from a song called 'Nature Boy': *The greatest thing you'll ever learn is just to love and be loved in return.*"

"'Nature Boy'?" she said. "Is that on the charts?"

"You bet. Nineteen forty-eight."

"Nineteen *forty-eight?* Who was *alive* then?"

"Oh, Jane Russell, John Coltrane, and lots of us dinosaurs."

Late one afternoon, another daughter of fifteen came to me and said, "Dad, what is love?"

Wishing she had asked me something easier, like *Where does space end?*, I said, "Well . . . it's a feeling . . . it may be what you're feeling right now with those eyes that keep saying, 'He hasn't called.'"

++

"How did you know?"

"I know that *something* has got you way down and it probably isn't the balance of trade."

"I'm in the pits."

"But this may just be a pit *stop*. What I mean is, you probably aren't really in *love*, you're just in *like.* "

"Dad, I'm fifteen, so I know an awful lot. And if this isn't love, then I don't know what love will ever be."

"It'll be what Mom and I have."

"You mean I'll turn out the light where he's sitting?"

"No, even more than that."

"I'll walk out of a room when he starts telling a story?"

"I'm afraid you haven't seen enough of the really wonderful side."

"I'm just teasing you."

"It's good you still have your sense of humor."

"If Larry doesn't call me, I'm going to lose it. He said if he didn't call me during the day, he'd definitely call me at nine tonight."

"I'll do everything I can to help," I said, wondering what that could be.

At eight o'clock, my daughter sat down beside the telephone as if she had come to an altar to pray.

"It's only eight o'clock, honey," I told her. "You said he's supposed to call at nine."

"He may have forgotten to change to Daylight Savings Time," she said. "He thinks of me so constantly that he can't concentrate on anything else. Would you please check the line?"

"Certainly, dear."

My years as a Navy medic had taught me the proper style for dealing with the insane, so I picked up the phone and dialed the operator.

"Hello, operator," I said. "Will you please tell the person in charge of this line that for the rest of the evening we want no calls from anyone not named Larry. But don't bother to put Olivier through."

For the next forty-five minutes, she kept her lonely vigil by the telephone, a girl in silent supplication to her flicking flame. At eight fifty-five, her brother came by, reached for the phone, and almost lost his hand.

"What's wrong with *her?*" he cried.

"She's fifteen," I said, saying it all.

At two minutes after nine, she said, "He may have moved to a different time zone. Dad, there are lots of places where it's not nine o'clock now, right?"

"Absolutely. In fact, it's not nine in more places than it is."

I was keeping her company down the rabbit hole.

"Or maybe he's under arrest," said her brother, "and he's used up his one phone call. Too bad you're not a lawyer."

+++

It took me longer than I had expected to pull her off him.

At five minutes after nine, I told her, "Remember something, honey: there are millions of guys out there," a bit of census-taking that I instantly realized was a mistake.

"Dad, that's one of the dumbest things you've ever said," she replied. "There's only *one* guy out there and I thought he cared."

"Well, just don't panic now. Your mother is always half an hour late with *me.*"

"I don't care how *old* people behave."

When Larry hadn't called by ten, she went up to her room with tears in her eyes and my heart followed her there. A few minutes later, I went to her.

"Are you all right?" I said.

"As all right as I can be," she said, "now that my life is over."

"Remember, you're just deeply in *like.* You can still be his friend, and a friend is someone you have forever."

"Dad, have you been reading fortune cookies? Larry was sent to me by *God.*"

"A special delivery, I admit, but what you have to decide now is this: Is it over or do you want to keep fighting for him? Is this just a practice run for marriage or is Larry really the person you want?"

"I just want him to *call* so I can tell him I never want to see him again."

"I know, honey," I said, suddenly remembering my own desire to use the telephone to destroy darling Charlene. "You're feeling rejected."

"Just because he doesn't call doesn't mean he's *rejecting me.*"

"Of course, of course. If he wanted to reject you, he'd probably call and . . ."

Feeling that both of us now had taken enough talk from the Mad Hatter, I gave her a goodnight kiss, perhaps the thing of greatest value from a father to a daughter of fifteen.

The following afternoon I was sitting in my living room, wondering how the wild geese decided which one would be the point man of the V, when the telephone rang and a young man asked for my wounded daughter.

"Who is this?" I said.

"Larry," he replied.

"Larry, this is Mr. Cosby. I'm afraid we've got a little problem."

"Can I help?"

"Absolutely: the problem is you. I hate to be the kind of father who meddles in his daughter's affairs with a boy, but I'm managing to overlook my hate. You see, Larry, I truly love my daughter more than I think you ever could and I don't want to see her hurt."

"Mr. Cosby, I—"

"So you just can't let her go on in a limbo like this. You've got to let her know exactly how you feel. I mean, if you just want to be her friend—a terrible word, I know—then you have to tell her that."

"Yes, sir. But you see—"

"I'm glad you understand. Now she'll be back in an hour, so make sure you call her then."

"Yes, sir," he said, sounding defeated, the state in which I wanted him.

"Good boy, Larry. Nice talking to you."

About an hour later my daughter returned and I was happy to be able to tell her, "Larry called."

"He *did?*" she said, lighting up.

"Yes, and . . . well, I didn't want to interfere in things, but . . . now this may seem like a mistake right *now,* but you'll really thank me for it in twenty or thirty years."

"Dad," she said, looking stricken, "what did you tell him? No, I don't want to know."

Nevertheless, I told her and she listened as if watching an accident. When I had finished, she softly said, "I'll be needing some change of address cards. I'm moving to Peru."

"But at least before you go you'll be finding out how he feels."

✛✛

"I *know* how he feels. He feels I have a very strange father."

"A very strange father who *cares*. Dear, I just wanted to help him say what's in his heart. Please forgive me."

"I guess I do."

"And please don't tell Mom. In some states, this would be grounds for divorce."

A little while later the telephone rang, she answered it upstairs, and I held my breath. When the conversation was over, she came thumping down the stairs and leaped the last two into the room, a huge smile on her face.

"That was Larry!" she said.

"And he wants to be more than a friend. *See*, a father's wisdom comes through again. The boy was just a little confused."

"Dad, he was more confused than a little. That was the *wrong Larry.*"

"You mean . . ."

"You asked him his plans for me and I'm afraid I don't fit in. He's going to be a priest."

I paused for a moment of introspection, and then I said, "I'll be the one going to Peru. You think Larry could send me off with a blessing?"

She laughed. "But you know, Dad, I've been thinking. If my father feels I'm in a situation I can't handle myself, then I must really be a jerkette."

❖❖

"A little jerk?" I said with a smile full of love.

"A big female one. So I've decided I'm going to Larry—"

"The lay Larry, you mean."

"Yes, and ask him some serious questions about where we are."

"And also tell him you have some wonderful genes on your mother's side. The side that has the keys to the house."

14

A WING AND A PRAYER

It was a small dinner party with two dear friends to celebrate our twenty-fifth anniversary and the talk had begun with such cosmic concerns as why men always leave toilet seats up.

"God knows how many women have drowned," said Camille. "And right after they worked so hard to take off all that weight."

"I married Dave because he doesn't leave the toilet seat up," said Caroline. "It may be his best quality."

"I wonder if the angle of the toilet seat is the secret of a happy marriage," I said, "or if there's more to it than that."

"There may be one more thing," said Caroline's husband, Dave. "I once read in a magazine that the way to keep a woman happily married is to suddenly sneak up on her and kiss the back of her neck."

+++

"*I've* done that!" I said, smiling triumphantly at Camille. "And here we are: twenty-five years. Should I switch to biting now? Or is that just for happy wives in Transylvania?"

"No," said Dave, "I think the article said you should do the biting on her ear—or blow on it or blow your nose before you sing to her; I really can't remember now."

"You just never know when and where to bite, blow, kiss, pat, or rub," I said. "Women should come with directions."

"Yes," said Camille, "and the first one should be to avoid men who learn to make love from *Popular Mechanics.*"

"I think it was *Gentlemen's Quarterly,*" said Dave.

"*Cattlemen's Quarterly,* you mean," said Camille. "But I don't care if it was the Dead Sea Scrolls. A woman isn't just a collection of buttons for a man to press, a collection of erotic knee jerks."

"You never say that when I'm giving you one of my great back rubs," I told her.

"That's true, I admit. You're one of the good hands people."

"And here we are. I've been rubbing you the right way and the wrong way and we've lasted twenty-five years. The League of *Nations* didn't last twenty-five years. The Oakland *Raiders* didn't last twenty-five years."

+++

"Only you and I and 'Gilligan's Island.' "

"I wonder if we've learned any rules for how to do this, maybe something we could put on stone tablets and have distributed at bus terminals and in public schools. For example, one important rule for a good marriage is to know each other's references."

"What do you mean by that?" said Camille.

"I mean I could only have married a woman who knew who John Coltrane was."

"Then you could have married Moms Mabley. But it's true, Caroline: I did have to pretend I knew John Coltrane and Harrison Willard."

"*Dillard.*"

"Whatever."

"You *faked* that?"

"Because I loved you and I knew it was important for you to think that I understood your sweaty world. Honey, women have been doing that ever since Eve left the rib cage to develop her own ID."

"I'll bet you never tested him on *your* references," said Caroline.

"Course not. Women have more sense than that."

"You've got references?" I said. "Okay, *try* me—anything from Jefferson Davis to Miles."

"All right, who was Alexander Fleming?"

"Easy! The first host of 'Jeopardy.' "

"The first host to invent penicillin. *Alexander* Fleming, not Art."

"Everybody gets them confused."

"Right, the same people who confuse Woodrow Wilson with Mookie."

"This may not be such a good idea," said Caroline as I felt the urge to test Camille's mind in a game of one-on-one. "Dear Abby just ran some tips for brides on how to have a successful marriage and one of them is: *Don't correct him in front of other people.*"

"Another is: *Don't give him Dear Abby's tips,*" said Dave.

"What were the others?" said Camille. "It's okay to say them; Bill never listens."

"I think I heard that," I said.

"Well, there was: *Don't threaten to leave him unless you have a better place to go* and *Don't tell him about all the other men you could have married* and . . . and *Don't show him the bills at breakfast.* And also: *Plan to be spontaneous and surprising.*"

"That's the one *I* like," I said to Camille. "Plan to be spontaneous and surprising. Like Pearl Harbor. Okay, here comes some planned spontaneity. Tomorrow I'm coming to dinner on roller skates. So don't make it buffet."

"Bill," said Caroline, "Abby just meant—"

"No, I think it's great that we now have all these rules for marriage. What's next? A commissioner's office? A three-point shot? Let's see, that would be kissing both cheeks and—"

"Calm down, dear," said Camille.

"If you two are going to fight," said Caroline, "do it creatively."

"You mean put our insults into couplets?" I said.

"No, I mean follow Dr. Aaron Beck's rules for no-fault fights."

"No-fault fights? Where'd you read *those?* In *Car and Driver?* Tell me, who's the marriage counselor for *Sports Afield?* I'd like to learn how to make love while swimming upstream."

"You've learned already." said Camille.

"Bill," said Caroline, "Dr. Beck is the father of cognitive therapy at the University of Pennsylvania."

"Well, I'm the father of five from Temple and we whipped Penn plenty when I was there."

"Not in cognitive therapy. For example, Dr. Beck says that while you're fighting creatively—"

"Like throwing paint at each other."

"—you should also schedule a ventilation session, especially if you're too hot."

Suddenly, in the midst of getting my master's in marriage, I looked at Camille and started to laugh.

"Ventilation session 'cause you're too hot," I said. "Remember how much you wanted a ventilation session when I dragged you into that sauna?"

"*Do* I," she said, also starting to laugh. "Of course, you already *had* ventilation: those holes in your head that made you want to have a barbecued wife."

+++

"Listen, it was *great* for you until you started to die. You lost more weight in five minutes in that sauna than you did in five *days* at that health farm."

"I should've stayed out of that place too."

"I *tried* to rescue you, but I couldn't get through the border guard."

"I wonder why. You had enough fat to pass the entrance exam—for a *scholarship*, in fact."

Shaking with laughter now, I said, "Camille, I never heard anything as poignant as your phone call pleading for the rescue."

"I was starting to eat pictures of meat."

"You could've tunneled out through the alfalfa."

"I probably could've *flown* out: everything I ate looked like bird seed!"

"Did you ever see the people who *sell* that health food? They look like the senior class on Devil's Island."

"That farm *was* Devil's Island—but without the fun."

There were tears in our eyes now, the kind that came whenever we were laughing in sync at some merry memory, the kind that helped to counteract divorce. At that giddy moment, I knew that the heart of marriage is memories; and if the two of you happen to have the same ones and can savor your reruns, then your marriage is a gift from the gods, whether your spontaneity is planned or spontaneous, whether you're using the *Kama Sutra* or *A Guide for Campfire Girls.*

"You see, David," I said, "there are no rules; you just have to wing it. A wing and a prayer, that's what marriage is. I don't care what Dear Abby says: *Camille* wouldn't mind if I brought out the bills at breakfast."

"Just as long as *one* Bill keeps cooking it," she sweetly said, and I lit a cigar, the kind I always have with my oatmeal.

15

THE PROMISED LAND

Grow old along with me!
The best is yet to be.

When Browning wrote these lines, he wasn't thinking of my mother and father or anyone else in North Philadelphia; but whenever I see my mother and father together, I know they're residing in a state where I want to live with Camille, a state of such blessed mellowness that they make the Dalai Lama seem like a Type A personality.

I will never forget my first awareness that my mother and father had ascended to a matrimonial plane where only God knew what they were doing—perhaps. We were driving to Philadelphia from Atlantic City, with my father at the wheel, my mother beside him, and me in the back.

"Oh, there's a car from Pittsburgh," said my mother, looking at a license plate in the next lane.

✦✦

"How do you know it's from Pittsburgh?" said my father.

"Because I couldn't think of Pennsylvania," she replied.

And I waited for my father to respond to this Einsteinian leap into another dimension, but he didn't speak. He simply continued to drive, a supremely contented man.

Because he had understood.

He had understood that my mother's Pittsburgh was a mythical place, located where the Monongahela entered the twilight zone. My mother also had not been able to think of Afghanistan, but she didn't say that the car was from Kabul. However, *had* she said that the car was from Kabul, my father would have understood it bore Afghans moving to Allentown.

For the next twenty minutes, I thought about fifty-three years of marriage and how they had bonded my parents in this remarkable Zen rapport; but then I was suddenly aware that my father had just driven past the exit for Philadelphia. Not the exit for Pennsylvania or for North America, but for Philadelphia, the literal city.

"Mom," I said, "didn't Dad just pass the exit we want?"

"Yes, he did," she replied.

"Well, why don't you *say* something?"

+++

"Your father knows what he's doing."

Had *I* driven past the proper exit, my wife would have said, *Please pull over and let me out. I'd like to finish this trip by hitching a ride on a chicken truck.*

But if Camille and I can just stay together another twenty-five years, then we also will have reached the Twilight Zone, where one of us will do something idiotic and the other one not only will understand it but admire it as well.

You turned out the light where I'm reading, I will tell her. *Thank you for the surprise trip to the planetarium.*

You left your shoes in the bathtub, she will tell me. *Thank you for giving me two more boats.*

One morning a few days after that memorably roundabout trip to Philadelphia, I got another glimpse of the lotus land where my parents dwelled. My father came into the house, took off his hat, put it on a chair, gave some money to my children, and then went back and sat on his hat.

"You just sat on your hat," my mother told him.

"Of course I did," he replied, and then neither one of them said another word about hat reduction. When the time came to leave, my father picked up the crushed hat and put it on his head, where it sat like a piece of Pop Art. My mother glanced at it, as if to make sure that it would not fall off, and then she took his arm and they walked out the door, ready to be the sweethearts of the Mummers Parade.

However, if *I* ever sat on my hat, Camille would say, *Can't you feel that you're sitting on your hat?*

And I would reply, *It's a tradition in my family for a man to sit on his hat. It's one of the little things that my father did for my mother.*

Yes, twenty-five years, happy as they have been, are still not enough to have given Camille and me that Ringling Brothers rhythm my mother and father enjoy. But we can hear the circus calling to us.

Love, what follies are committed in thy name, said Francis Bacon.

So far, most of marriage has been the Ziegfeld Follies for Camille and me. And now we're getting ready to send in the clowns.

BOOK MARK

*This book was composed in
the typefaces Aster and Keller
Antiqua by Berryville Graphics,
Berryville, Virginia*

*It was printed and bound
by Orange Graphics,
Orange, Virginia*

DESIGNED BY CAROL MALCOLM

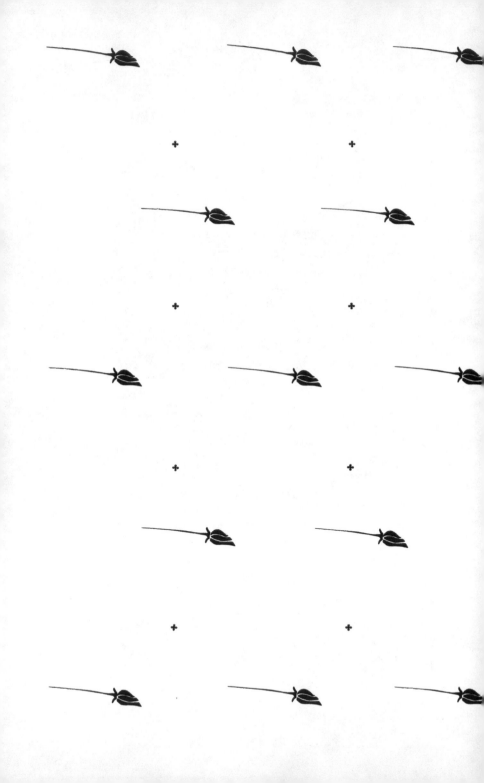

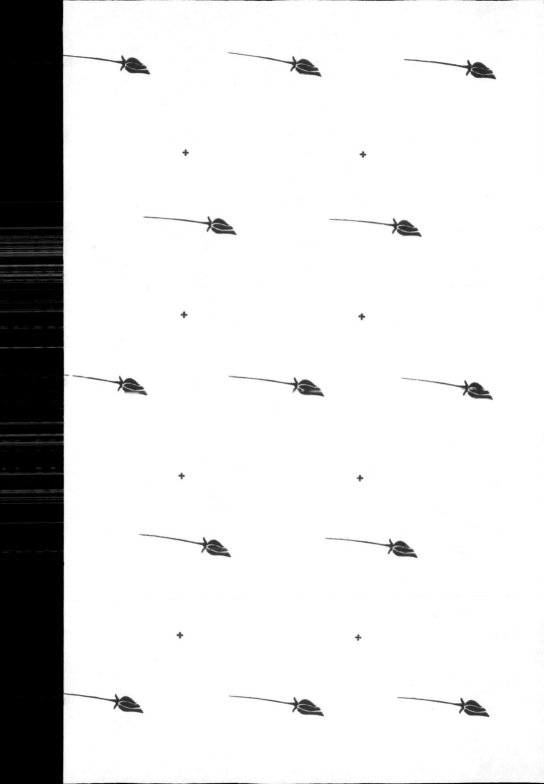